WHY DO GOATS CLIMB TREES?

AN OVERLAND TRAVELLER'S TALES IN AFRICA

JAMES MARR

latitude14.com

COPYRIGHT

Published by Latitude14 Publishing
www.latitude14.com
First published in 2007 by Grosvenor House publishing Ltd

The CIP catalogue record for this book is available at the British Library.
ISBN 978-1-7384756-2-9 ebook
ISBN 978-1-7384756-6-7 paperback

CONTENTS

track we've bucked and rattled along for most of the day, it's not something you'd undertake lightly.

The lakes in question are named Tislit and Iseli, and they are found high up in Morocco's Atlas Mountains. According to local lore, they are lovers, betrothed since the dawn of time, and they are destined to long for each other eternally, for the hand of nature has ensured they can never be joined together. Which suggests our fleet-footed pyromaniac is playing quite the gooseberry. It's probably just as well there's an abundance of water, considering his penchant for self-ignition.

'Is it okay if we camp under these trees?' JP asks, breaking the silence.

The guardian beams at us, throwing open his arms. Clearly our integrity is not for a moment in question.

Pete scowls in the direction of Wandy. 'At least there're no windsocks next to this lake, eh, Swales?'

Wandy Swales nonchalantly taps the upended bowl of his pipe against a tree. The fluttering ash clings to his trousers, and he pats it into a grey smudge. 'How was I to know we'd camped at the end of an airstrip?' he parries good-naturedly.

'Unless I'm greatly mistaken, you were, in fact, the navigator.'

In the darkness of the previous night, we'd inadvertently strayed onto a grass airstrip. It had been the end of a long day on the road, and we were keen to get our heads down. A local pilot gave us the fright of our lives at first light, the Cessna's wheels barely clearing the roof of our Land Rover as it swooped in to land. I gaze about me from beneath this cluster of trees where we're standing and look across the glimmering lake. This is a different proposition altogether.

1

A SOJOURN IN THE SAHARA

1988

We're not sure where he's sprung from this spare, winded fellow, his lungs whistling like a ruptured bellows.

'He's asking for a smoke,' JP says, his outstretched hand offering an open packet of Lucky Strike.

The man snatches a cigarette, his other hand hustling a brass lighter from his jacket pocket. He holds it to the tobacco, scattering a shower of sparks – click, click – WHUMP!

I flinch when his head briefly vanishes beyond a ball of flame. Lucky Strike, indeed.

Inhaling blissfully on the charred remains, a tendril of smoke leaks from his left nostril when he croaks, 'I'm the guardian of these lakes.'

The guardian of these lakes? We each of us exchange a bemused look, nobody willing to question our visitor on why they need protecting. Or from whom? How in the world might you steal a lake from up here? Judging by the

ALSO BY THE AUTHOR

Fiction

KILL AT FIRST LIGHT

Non-fiction

SHORT STORIES FROM A LONG CONTINENT

The Americas Overland

CITY OF MYTHS, RIVER OF DREAMS

The Road to Timbuktu

WHY DO GOATS CLIMB TREES?

An Overland Traveller's Tales in Africa

and I share a room in a decaying hotel. I strip off and jump eagerly under the shower. The taps screech when I turn them, producing an intermittent drip. Turning both taps fully to the right does no more than prolong this irksome noise.

'I could be some time, guys,' I shout at the closed door.

BY LATE AFTERNOON the next day, we're back at Figuig, standing in front of the same border official with our crispy insurance papers obtained in Oujda. He looks mildly peeved at our tenacity, swatting us beyond the raised pole with barely a glance.

From here, we cross no man's land and enter Algeria without too much fuss. It costs us a calculator and a couple of worn music cassettes – *George Benson's Greatest Hits* and an old Bob Marley album. Having overexposed ourselves to George and Bob on the long roads in Morocco, all of us agree we can get by without another rendition of "Buffalo Soldier" or "Give Me the Night".

We eat at a roadside café and, exhausted, camp out on the edge of the wonderfully named Grand Erg Occidental. We discuss how to make the most suitable bed on a plain consisting of baked earth and fist-sized rocks. I kick away some of the rocks, scallop out the ground with a shovel and lie in it, shuffling my shoulders to smooth out the rough edges. With a sleeping bag and a jacket for a pillow, this is about as good as it's going to get.

I drift off to sleep, blissfully ignorant of what lies in store for us tomorrow.

. . .

It's midmorning, and four Algerian soldiers surround us, their weapons jigging back and forth. We're under arrest, crouched in the sand by the side of the road to Adrar, in full sunlight. It's unbearably hot, the sort of heat that very soon renders you a gibbering moron. If this continues much longer, I reckon our parlous situation will become entirely incidental, as I fear my brain is about to dribble out of my ears.

After rummaging through our luggage, the commandant is gesticulating menacingly. He's eager to learn why Pete possesses two passports. We all are, for that matter.

'I'm entitled to two passports!' he snaps defiantly.

Wandy leans towards him and utters, sotto voce, 'You didn't have to bring them both, old man.'

'Nonsense!'

JP does his best to appease the commandant. The soldier's bushy moustache bristles, and I suspect, whatever he's being told, it's not going to plan. We stand accused of being imperialist spies. A mercenary force bent on dark deeds. By all accounts, it seems a long spell in prison is the least we can expect. I swallow drily, not just because of this heat. I've heard bad things about Algerian prisons – and it's nothing to do with the food they serve, either. After Wandy's cooking, I feel sufficiently fortified to tackle anything. My growing fear concerns another matter altogether. I have a *Lawrence of Arabia* moment: his abduction by the Turks, that scene in the film when... no, let's not go there.

Our captors search the Land Rover more closely for the weapons they're convinced we're carrying, in the process uncovering the stash of miniature bottles of spirit. Their lips quiver, and JP seizes the opportunity. He sidles forward with all the sang-froid of an over-zealous air steward, offloading handfuls of Drambuie and Gordon's London Dry Gin. A shifty grin, suggestive of illicit pleasure and profit, divides the commandant's face. Perhaps we're not mercenaries, after all. He dispatches one of his men to fetch a sack from their jeep. Accompanied by much clinking of glass, they fill it, and the soldiers' rifles are quietly put away.

Hurrah!

Tongue lolling, I claw my way into the shade. Having struck such an agreeable trade, we all celebrate with a pot of green tea and discuss the best route to Tamanrasset.

An hour later, we stop by a fallen acacia tree. I must admit, I haven't seen a tree for some time. 'We'll take some wood,' JP announces. 'This might be our last opportunity.'

We set about breaking up the acacia, using the tyre levers to crack apart the solid branches and humping the wood onto the roof rack. Lunch is a tin of sardines, some bread and a top-up of the suntan.

We hit the desert town of Adrar by late afternoon and enter through an impressive archway. In search of supplies, we discover a warehouse on the edge of town. The locals appear more than a little interested in us. It's not just me; we all sense the hostility in the air. We are to learn how rioting has broken out in the major northern towns of Algeria concerning commodity shortages and high prices. The demonstrations are being encouraged by Islamist groups inspired by the intifada, the uprising of Palestinians against Israeli rule on the West Bank of the Jordan River and the Gaza Strip. Over the next few days, troops will kill five hundred demonstrators and arrest three and a half thousand more. This is not a great time to be in Algeria.

At the entrance to the warehouse a Tuareg sits astride his couched camel, a rifle cradled in his arms. His face is so weathered by the elements it has more folds to it than a prune. Only his beady eyes move. The camel slowly works his jaws, chewing something it appears decidedly reluctant to swallow.

The Tuareg are probably the best-known nomads of the Sahara, if only for their traditional indigo robes. They are said to be descendants of the Berber from the north-west, where they lived a quiet, civilised existence until routed by the Arabs over a thousand years ago. They migrated to the central Sahara, controlling the trans-Saharan trade routes, allegedly practising their own brand of racketeering and robbery. Having failed in more recent times to establish autonomy for themselves, today they live in the desert regions of what are now Algeria, Mali, Niger and Libya. They are made up of several regional clans, each speaking a different dialect of Tamasheq, the Tuareg language, and have mildly differing customs and dress. Collectively, they call themselves Kel Tagelmust, 'the people of the veil'. The name Tuareg is said to originate from an Arabic, and less noble, designation – 'abandoned by the gods'.

Inside the warehouse, the shelves are almost empty. There are row upon row of conical-shaped blocks of sugar. If you painted orange bands around them, they could double as traffic cones. Not that there's much call for traffic cones out here, edible or otherwise. There is also an abundance of red paint, stacked beside catering-sized tins of strawberry jam. And that's it. I think even the village idiot might grasp why there's such unrest in this country. With little use for the red paint, we settle for a cone of sugar and a tin of jam.

Outside, the camel is still chewing whatever it was chewing when we went inside, and youths have clustered beside our car, observing us with a degree of hostility. Even though we'd effortlessly pass muster at a vagrants' line-up and that the Land Rover might be mistaken for a tinker's truck sprouting crooked acacia limbs, I've no doubt this gathering only sees a bunch of decadent Europeans. I'm sorry for their predicament. We are lucky to be able to drive away. And we do. At the edge of town, we top up the water container from a standpipe and don't hang around.

We camp well out of town and strike up a fire. Tonight, to apportion mutual blame, we each take our part in the cooking process. While there is absolutely no improvement in the standard of cuisine, it does serve to keep relations on an even keel. After eating, we each take a few moments to grumble to ourselves and then all is well.

At this point in the journey, JP promises to make couscous, his signature dish from the tour guiding days in Mali. I'd like to think his proposal is a real morale booster, but I'm still in two minds. I've seen the photographs of those trips he used to make.

As we enjoy the fire, Pete recounts his time in the army. He and Wandy first met while serving in the Ulster Defence Regiment. Later in his army career, Pete was sent to Kenya during the Mau Mau uprising, a rebellion staged mainly by the Kikuyu tribe who resented British Colonial rule and the land grab by British settlers. He was quickly despatched into the bush to protect the inhabitants of remote villages from Mau Mau raiding parties.

'Our rules of engagement had been clear,' he recalls in uncharacteristically hushed tones. 'We had orders to shoot the buggers.'

As he continues with the story, I can tell that whatever took place all those years ago has deeply affected him.

'Our NCO used to shout at us: "You kill them because they'll sure as hell kill you if you don't."'

One night, in all the confusion, it seems one of the womenfolk of the village was accidentally shot and killed, sadly mistaken for a Mau Mau guerrilla advancing on the soldiers' position.

'We were sent to bloody well help them,' Pete murmurs, after a moment's silence.

THE TARMAC ROAD runs out shortly after Reggane. We head east on the desert piste in the direction of In Salah. This is my first experience of desert driving. And it's bewildering. This barren plain is akin to an ocean. There are no external references to seek guidance from and nothing on which to focus. I'm constantly glancing at the compass arrow bobbing wildly in its sphere of liquid. Beyond the windscreen, the white heat and the dust reduce the horizon to a distorted, shimmering image that exists in the near distance: soft sand, dry riverbeds, sunken ground – all hazards demanding a constant deviation from course. And there is always the temptation to follow the criss-crossing tyre tracks of other vehicles. JP does his best to keep me on the straight and narrow. My concentration is absolute.

We stop after a while to make tea, and JP chooses this moment to release a strange creature he's been keeping quiet from us. It has four legs, no head and a texture similar to a fossilised wash leather. He calls it a guerba.

'She's a goatskin,' he imparts matter-of-factly. 'And she's been dead for years.'

'I'd have never guessed,' Pete quips, cautiously poking it with a finger. 'At least we don't have to feed it.'

We name it 'The Thing', and when JP fills it with water from a container, I'm fascinated by how the crusty hide bloats and flicks into shape – FLICK! goes one leg... FLICK! goes another. Finally, having slaked its thirst, I wonder if this creature might miraculously spring into life, like a ruminant version of Frankenstein. Having tied it to the roof rack, The Thing is left to hang down the side of the Land Rover.

'She'll stay cool enough here,' JP murmurs, patting her wobbly belly.

'It leaks a lot,' I say.

'That's okay. The evaporation keeps the water cool.'

'You call that evaporation?' Pete runs a hand through his hair. 'It's more like a frigging colander.'

Wandy chews thoughtfully on the stem of his pipe before uttering, 'She's no looker, is she?'

'Get a grip, Swales. You've only been out here a week.' Pete strides forward and flicks The Thing's belly. 'Which end do you drink from then, JP?'

'I tell you, my friend. When your life depends on it, the water tastes just as sweet from either end.'

Pete holds up his thumb and forefinger, barely a gap between them. 'I'd have to be that close to death before I described anything coming out of this bugger as sweet.'

It's become impossible to remain out of the car any longer. A light wind is whipping this ugly, black grit into our eyes and ears. It crunches in my teeth. And a swarm of gnats are constantly biting us. The heat is intensely aggravating. Where are the golden dunes? The blue sky? So far, this place is my version of hell. We pack away our kettle and cups and clamber back aboard.

Arriving in In Salah by early evening, we treat ourselves to a room in the local hotel. It's pretty comfortable. I take a shower. When I'm nicely covered in soap, the flow of water becomes an intermittent drip. Ugh! Does all the plumbing out here revert to only one setting?

. . .

After In Salah, we head south to Tamanrasset. The road is mostly a thing of the past. Vast swathes of tarmac have been swallowed by the desert or torn apart in great slabs. We follow tracks weaving off into the desert, though remaining roughly parallel with the old road. We make slow progress. There's very little traffic – the occasional truck looms towards us from the south. Finally, we pass golden sand dunes off to our left.

After some hours, we stop for a break, and Rolf stalks a flock of doves with his bow and arrow. He crouches low, the arrow partially drawn in the bow. Full of expectation, I video the hunt. But it's not to be. The birds take flight, the released arrow striking a rock, snapping in half. So, I guess we must eat vegetables... again. I'm also tired of tinned pilchards and sardines, our lunchbreak staple. The bonnet, which has come to double as our kitchen worktop, is now caked in discarded fish bones, tomato sauce and brine. Even from a couple of paces, it emits quite a whiff. I'm not looking forward to cleaning it.

A little further on lies an abandoned hermit's hut. The guidebook advises all travellers to circle it three times for good luck, and so we do. Taking a break, we wander inside, discovering that travellers have scrawled messages and slapped stickers on the walls. There's a photograph of a party of kids from Sedbergh School in the north of England. I recognise some of them. It's a small world.

After we've made camp, I use the water purifier to filter a fresh batch of well water, pouring it into our clean jerry can and then dropping in a couple of sterilizing tablets, just for good measure. Considering these conditions, I'm very keen for my plumbing department to function as well as one might hope. JP laughs at me scornfully before taking a long draught from The Thing. It's still dripping in several places, leaving me to speculate if he might have dispatched the goat with his shotgun rather than his knife. The dripping water has soaked the front of his shirt. Standing here flaunting a guerba instead of a parrot, he reminds me of some half-demented pirate. Having already divulged his preferred method for settling his stomach prior to such a trip as this (eating the most fly-blown meat he can find in Algeciras' open market), he now appears at liberty to consume whatever he wishes, from wherever he wishes.

'I'm telling you,' he cackles, 'this is the best water you'll drink.'

'May I try it?' asks Wandy, never one to shirk a challenge.

We all stop whatever we are doing, unable to avert our eyes from this unfolding drama. Now, in my mind, Wandy's something of a tough guy. He's served with both the Royal Marines and the Parachute Regiment, spending a good slice of his life wandering the jungles of Indonesia, drinking from swamps and eating caterpillars. Wandy's a boxer, has climbed the Matterhorn and played rugby for London Irish – there's no way an old goat skin is going to faze a fellow of his resolute nature. After a few deep breaths, he puts the guerba to his lips and gulps. Within the tick of the cooling engine, he explodes like a geyser. His tongue flicks, lizard-like, back and forth across his lips, and he groans softly. 'What the blazes did it eat before you killed it?'

JP offers a Gallic shrug. 'Maybe she's been in the garage a bit too long.'

Feeling more than a little smug, I down a mouthful from the jerry can and instantly gasp for air. It's as if I'm drowning in an overheated, over-chlorinated swimming pool. I keep such opinions to myself. (Perhaps I should only use one sterilizing tablet next time.)

. . .

By late morning the next day, we arrive in Tamanrasset, a significant trading town in the Sahel. We go for a wander, buying food supplies in the market, including chunks of dodgy-looking lamb meat for the couscous JP still threatens to make.

Next up is the tailor, from whom we acquire lengths of black cloth to make a shesh, a head-cloth or veil, and JP and the tailor give us a lesson in how they must be worn. Tuareg chic determines how much cloth should be wound around the head and how much should fall from the shoulder. We take a while to get this just right. Does vanity know no bounds? Suitably attired, there's a new purpose in our step as we swagger back to the Land Rover with our goods – to a man, we now consider ourselves Masters of the Desert. In truth, I suspect we look ridiculous.

We leave Tam and take the track to the plateau of Assekrem in the Hoggar Mountains. After a couple of hours, we make camp, and JP tinkers with the Land Rover, changing the engine oil and filter. When he's finished, his hands are as black as the night sky.

'I'll make the lamb couscous next,' he announces.

Having by now eaten our way through the equivalent of a medium-sized vegetable patch, this is truly cause for celebration – cause enough for a drink, if only the commandant with the bushy moustache hadn't nicked it all. Nevertheless, my belly is rumbling with anticipation. After a while, Pete steps up to the bonnet, where JP's hands disappear into a metal bowl.

'Why's the semolina so dark?' he asks.

JP squints when he looks up. 'I don't know, Pete,' he says. 'But my hands have never been cleaner.'

'Anyone still for couscous?' Wandy declares.

THE TRACK to the plateau of Assekrem is slow going in the Land Rover. The highest peak in this range, Mount Tahat, stands just short of three thousand metres high. The route on the map is about as long as my little finger, yet we've been at it for hours. Finally, we leave the car and proceed on foot up a narrow track at the end of which is the tiny hermitage established by Count Charles de Foucauld – the Hermit of the Hoggar. I stop to take in the view of the mountains. Fluted volcanic plugs rise above the plateau like contorted stalagmites, their distinctive form deflecting the sunlight and casting ghostly shadows over the basalt ranges. It is truly an austere site. Inside the stone hut is an altar, a crucifix, and some of the count's books. While here, he compiled a French–Tamasheq dictionary and a comprehensive collection of Tuareg poetry.

Born in Strasbourg in 1858, Charles de Foucauld was educated at the Military School of Saint Cyr and the Cavalry School of Saumur, where he acquired a certain notoriety as a bon viveur. He distinguished himself in the campaign at Oran, a coastal town in the north-west of Algeria, in 1881, before becoming subsumed into the Arab culture and way of life. De Foucauld came to Tamanrasset in 1905 and built this hermitage on the plateau five years later. I sit outside his hut wondering what drove him to this place. What, ultimately, was he seeking? For all his good work in the local community, he was killed by marauders in 1916.

We camp at the foot of the plateau. Rolf sleeps beneath a shelter of rocks. In the morning, he wakes surrounded by scorpions. Fortunately, they're friendly ones.

. . .

We rise early to catch the dawn light. It's an eerie and stunning landscape that creeps from the darkness, and the track down is slow and arduous. Back in Tamanrasset, we head north until reaching a village going by the name of Tit. We must clear our south-westerly passage with the local police, for ahead of us lies one thousand two hundred kilometres of barren desert, all the way to the Malian border.

As soon as we pull up in Tit, Pete, who's a tad off-colour, leaps from the vehicle.

'There's a more suitable part of the human anatomy to call this place,' he rumbles, mincing to the cover of a low wall.

JP and I amble to the police station, this sun sucking the life from us; my skin tightens, searing under its intensity. Unsurprisingly, for this time of the day, the streets are deserted. Inside the police station, half the desert seems to have washed through the door. The sand crunches beneath our boots, forming a small dune at the foot of the counter on which an ashtray overflows with cigarette butts – and more sand. A curtain covering the entrance to a back room flaps in the breeze. Curiously, a calendar on the wall depicts Highland cattle in a blizzard. We both of us gawp at it.

'Perhaps it's a form of therapy for the employees,' I venture.

From the back room, the creaking of bed springs precedes the arrival of the duty officer. His face has all the appearance of a crumpled paper bag.

'We're going to Timeiaouine,' JP tells him.

The bobby's eyelids rise and fall with the speed of a moth-eaten theatre curtain. He manages to raise an arm, at the end of which is a crooked finger. 'You want to end up like them?' he asks, pointing at the wall.

We turn to our left and face the montage of

photographs. I step closer. There's a 4x4 with its doors open. Equipment lies strewn in the sand. The dark mounds are bodies. There are two more pictures like this one – more bodies. Beneath these photos, there's one of a guy trapped beneath his fallen motorbike. His face is turned away from the camera, a film of sand covering his jacket.

'We've got plenty of water,' JP says.

Outside the police station, the bobby gives our vehicle a cursory glance. He looks at the sky and shrugs. 'Inshallah,' he utters before retreating inside.

Abalessa, a settlement not far to the south-west of us, is said to have been the southernmost Roman outpost in Africa. A tomb in Abalessa, excavated in the early 1920s, is also considered the burial site of Tin Hinan, Queen of the Kel Rega Tuaregs. According to legend, around the 4th century AD, this Berber princess made the desperate journey on foot across the desert from Tafilalet in Morocco, accompanied only by her faithful slave girl, Takama. As a consequence of such courage, she was chosen to be queen of the local tribes.

The thought of walking all the way here like Tin Hinan makes me shudder. Such a story amply places our own efforts in perspective.

An hour or so out of Tit, we follow a dry river, weaving between thorn scrub. A gazelle breaks cover, and we eagerly give chase. Long after the gazelle has shaken us, we're still discussing how it might best be served. We agree it shouldn't include semolina. And no vegetables.

As we trundle along, JP keeps looking up at the sun, our principal means of navigation. Using the sun and being mindful to avoid the patches of deep sand, he indicates the direction by flicking his hand – left a bit... right a bit... straight a bit.

'Shouldn't there be a track somewhere?' Wandy enquires, diligently following JP's instructions. I'm amused by how Wandy steers the Land Rover with exaggerated turns on the wheel, as if he's in a boat tackling a heavy sea.

'Yeah, a track would be nice,' JP agrees. His hand flicks again. 'Right a bit... left a bit...'

We crash through another dry riverbed. Pete's lying in the back, groaning and holding his stomach. A fine grey dust seeps through the tiniest of cracks, gradually suffocating us. The temperature inside the vehicle is blisteringly high. My skin prickles everywhere.

'So, where is it then, this track?' Wandy presses.

JP shoots him a sideways glance. 'I guess the sand must have covered it,' he says.

Eventually, we find a track, though the surface is badly corrugated. To minimise the hammering on the suspension, we must maintain an optimum speed of about eighty kilometres per hour to skim across the ridges. Cornering like this is like driving on ice. On a bend, the Land Rover skitters sideways. In response, Wandy heaves the wheel to starboard, pipe clamped in his teeth, the salty-seadog at work. Smoke billows from his pipe, and his knuckles are bone-white. It's all very alarming.

Oh, Lord! Here comes another corner.

Later, and we're back in thorn scrub and soft sand, the speed more controllable. There is a confusion of wheel marks. Further still, an escarpment fills the shimmering horizon. Suffering a moment of indecision, we stop and get out. Do we go around the escarpment to the north or to the south? JP cranes his neck and looks at the sun. South? North?

'We'll have a cup of tea,' he suggests.

Later, we find a dip in the escarpment and the Land

Rover scrabbles up the incline. The sand is hard-packed now. And it goes on for ever and ever – sand and sky – sky and sand – like the biggest beach I've ever seen. We can do more than one hundred kilometres per hour on this. There is absolutely nothing in any direction.

'Slow down!' Rolf calls out. He's staring intently into the white heat. 'Somebody is out there.'

Far to our left, a man is walking. Two camels follow him. I steer in their direction. As we draw closer, I see the nomad has nothing but the clothes he stands in. There are no supplies on the camels. He takes the cup of water we give him and tells us he's heading north. I find this almost unbelievable.

'But there's nothing to the north,' I say.

'Sure there is,' JP replies.

'I know there isn't,' I counter, 'because I've looked at the map.'

'Ah, forget about the map. That's just a piece of paper. This man holds all the knowledge he needs in his head.'

We bid the nomad farewell and, for a while, watch him on his way.

The sun is starting to fall now. Time to make camp. As we motor onward, we table a debate as to where we should stop. In that open space there? Or this one over here?

It's like trying to settle the age-old challenge of choosing where to park in an empty car park. The task is overwhelming, and we charge over the sand while the debate descends into bickering. Rolf retreats out of the window and goes to sit on the roof. Pete groans unintelligibly.

A tree gradually materialises from the haze. It must be the only tree for hundreds of kilometres.

'There's the Tree of Inspiration,' I declare, rather inanely.

'It's an acacia tree. Too many thorns.'

'I'm not mending a puncture.'

'Keep going a bit further.'

'We'll stop near the tree,' I announce. It's my car, after all.

The motion is carried.

In the falling light, we unpack the Land Rover and start a fire, careful not to tread on any nail-like acacia thorns on the ground. Pete's stomach cramps have still not left him. He is desperate to relieve himself – except there's nothing to hide behind. The deepest undulation comes from our tyre tracks. He must wait until darkness if he wants privacy. He decides he can wait, killing time by shuffling around the Land Rover searching for distraction. Before long, he's weaving at the back door, pulling on a metal chain for all he's worth. The rest of us observe his antics from beside the fire.

'You all right, Pete?' Wandy calls.

Suddenly, the chain and what it's attached to break free from the bowels of the vehicle. He slings it to the ground.

'God in heaven,' he groans. 'Can someone tell me what the hell we're doing with an anchor in all this frigging sand?'

Sunset finally arrives; the fire radiates a soft glow. The acacia tree seemingly dances in the fire's flickering light, the shadow of its twisted trunk performing a silent jig on the sand. Beyond the fire, the darkness spreads unhindered like the depths of an ocean, and the unblemished night sky is a mass of stars. Occasionally, it's disturbed by a streak of dazzling light as one breaks free on its reckless journey across the Galaxy.

. . .

DURING BREAKFAST, we're still weighing up the pros and cons of bringing the anchor.

'It's for pulling ourselves from deep sand,' I explain for the umpteenth time. 'We attach the winch to the chain, bury the anchor in the sand and, hey presto. It's in all the desert survival books.'

Nobody wants to listen to reason. When it's time to leave, Pete climbs onto the bonnet, salutes, and pipes us aboard.

We've left the firm ground long behind us now. We're back among the soft sand and thorn scrub. We passed one truck this morning; two men were changing a punctured tyre. When we stop for a break we find a camel bone bleached white by the sun. We tie it to the winch on the front as a lucky mascot. We grumble about who should sit in the front and who should sit in the back, like kids on a school outing. We travel in the vehicle for upwards of ten hours a day, so tension does set in from time to time. The smallest thing can irritate. Reality is such that nobody can drop out – you can't catch the bus out of here. We're in this together. The Land Rover and what it carries is our lifeline and our Achilles' heel. The further we go, the more I grasp how totally dependent we are upon it. It's not a feature to dwell on. I think of the nomad and his two camels. JP was right. What freedom. What knowledge. One has only to experience the harshness of this land to be humbled by this man.

We arrive at a tiny settlement made up of a handful of huts, a place JP has been talking of visiting for old time's sake. There's a bicycle leaning against one of the huts, a butcher's bike with a basket on the front. A spring pokes through the leather seat, and several spokes are missing from the wheels.

'Let's see if Mokti's in,' JP says.

He leads the way to one of the huts, knocking on a bleached wooden door. A tall man swathed head to toe in blue robes answers. Mokti's very pleased to see JP. It's been a long time, by all accounts, and they're old business partners.

'What sort of business were you both involved in?' I ask, entering the cool, dark hut.

'This and that,' JP replies dismissively.

By all accounts, Mokti is a hustler who travels the length and breadth of the desert, from Timbuktu in the west to northern Niger in the east.

'Surely he doesn't travel with that old butcher's bike?' says Wandy.

JP clicks his tongue. 'Of course not. He's got a camel. And a four-wheel drive.'

Mokti is a veritable barometer of Tuareg politics. We have several rounds of mint tea, and he brings JP up to date. It turns out all is not well. The state borders set by the colonialists are causing further division for the Tuareg communities spread throughout the Sahel. They have no county to call their own. Once again, they feel threatened, this time by the black African from the south.

'Soon there will be fighting,' Mokti says.

Mokti's brother is lying in the corner, shivering under the covering of blankets, apparently afflicted with malaria.

After the tea, we top up with fuel from the jerry cans on the roof and move on.

Tonight, we camp among low dunes. I imagine I will never forget these nights camping in the desert. As I lie here in the open, there is a light breeze; it is never too cold. The boundlessness and silence lend the desert a purity I've never before experienced in any place.

. . .

AT A SETTLEMENT, we take fuel from an old pump. In case it's dirty, we put it in the jerry cans, from where we can filter it later. With full fuel tanks, we head for the well outside the settlement where, among a small group of men, there's a donkey with barrels loaded across his back. The opening to the well is surrounded by wooden boards that flex as a wizened man heaves on a rope with a water container attached at the end, looking a lot like The Thing –quite possibly a distant relative. The man empties the water into the barrels on the donkey's back and starts over again. He's almost got the guerba back to the top when the rope parts with a thwack, followed seconds later by the smack of the full guerba hitting the surface of the water. The man pulls up what's left of the rope and plays the frayed strands between his fingers. He puts me in mind of a poker player lamenting a rotten hand. We crowd around the opening, peering down. It's very dark in the well, and the man doesn't have another guerba.

'They say truth is found at the bottom of a well,' Pete mutters as we gaze at the dark water. He shuffles awkwardly when we all look at him.

'And guerbas,' growls JP.

'I have an idea,' I say. I go to the car to fetch the anchor and a length of rope. 'We'll get it back for him with this.'

I'm feeling rather pleased with myself.

'Stand aside, Pete. You're blocking the light.' After much effort, I hook the guerba with one of the anchor's flukes and drag it back up. 'Who says an anchor is useless in the desert?'

We refill our containers with brown, gritty water and, in exchange, donate the rope to the village. It seems a fair trade.

. . .

Today, we're heading north on the Tanezrouft, the north–south desert highway. The sand is firm. We pass a couple of vehicles in the opposite direction, heading for Mali. We stop at the Tropic of Cancer, marked by a metal sign covered in graffiti. We park under the sign and take a lot of photos for Wandy's new brochure. It's somewhere around here that France tested their first atomic bomb, though we can't find any big holes. The route is littered with the skeletons of vehicles that never made it, many of them trucks.

That night, we camp away from the main thoroughfare after JP tells us how a truck once ploughed through someone's camp. At night, the trucks tend to drive by the moon and starlight only.

Nobody comes our way tonight. I watch satellites travel silently through the stars. Later, I dream of a warm shower. Clean clothes. Steak and chips. A glass of chilled beer.

The following day is to deliver a grievous blow to JP.

We stop late morning for a tea break to discover The Thing has slipped its tether and vanished. As we can't be sure when this occurred, we have a show of hands to determine whether to go back and conduct a search. Not surprisingly, the result is a resounding four against one, and we continue our journey north. Out of respect, a day of mourning is declared.

We tread carefully around JP. He's clearly gutted by the end of a beautiful friendship.

Crossing back into Morocco at Figuig, we make camp on a stony plain, but the moment we get bedded down, the heavens open. There isn't room for us all to sleep in the car, so we pack up and continue driving through the night. We've already done twelve hours today. The last thing I want to do is drive through the night, but we press on until dawn.

By midmorning we reach Ketama, a small town in the Rif Mountains. The place is surrounded by pine forests with an eerie mist clinging to the trees. This is a weird place, quite possibly because it is the heart of Morocco's cannabis-growing region. We've been followed for the last half hour by a big black Mercedes straight out of a gangster movie. It stops every time we do. When we pull over in the main street of Ketama, so does the Mercedes. When we get out, so do the heavies. They slouch around their car, eyeing us.

Bleary-eyed, hungry and tired, we saunter across the street and enter a bar. Inside, it's like a freak show. On benches along the walls are men in kaftans, the pointed hoods pulled over their heads. Their faces are partly masked by shadow, the air is sickly sweet from the hash they're smoking, and their vacant eyes follow us across the room. They're like something out of *A Nightmare on Elm Street*. It's wall-to-wall Freddie Krueger in here. We drink a coffee and take our chances with the heavies outside.

Back on the road, and the heavies continue following us. On a quiet stretch, they make their move, swerving the Mercedes in front of the Land Rover in an attempt to cut us off. Big mistake! What they fail to appreciate is that Captain Wandy is at the helm. He's had a whole night of lost sleep to vent on these creeps. He spins the wheel to port and rings on the power, forcing the Mercedes to take evasive action. There's a barking of tyres and a puff of blue smoke as the big black saloon slithers into the roadside, and the heavies finally give up.

'Damn ruffians,' Wandy mutters, tapping the bowl of his

pipe on the open window. A flurry of red cinders fills the car.

We take the ferry from Tangier to Algeciras. Upon arrival at the port, the Spanish customs pull us aside. They order us out of the vehicle and send in a slobbering dog. No sooner does the dog jump in than he leaps out again, whimpering and carrying his tail between his legs. Poor thing. It's hardly the picture of hygiene in there.

For a start, there's a pair of Pete's socks hanging from the roof, one bent at a right angle, in the final stages of rigor mortis. The customs man waves us through. He's looking at the bonnet as we pass, nostrils furiously twitching. I guess he's wondering if that fishy smell is legal or not.

We go to a restaurant I've been dreaming of for the past few days. They do big juicy steaks and piles of greasy chips. We pull up outside and clamber down. Amazingly, the bleached camel bone is still attached to the winch.

'She did us proud, the old girl.' I run a loving hand over the bonnet. It's like stroking barnacles. A young couple eye us warily as they leave the restaurant, hurrying to their car. I knock some of the Saharan dust from my shirt and swagger inside for a cold beer. Perhaps we really are Masters of the Desert. I spend a moment thinking of the nomad and his two camels out there, deep in the Sahara, and I check my stride.

2

DELIVERANCE

There's nothing quite like the primeval roar of a lion to chill the blood. All four of us spun round at the sound, confronted by a young male barely metres from the trail we'd cut through the tall grasses. We closed together, ever so slowly, eyeing this magnificent creature. The lion, in turn, observed the humans encroaching on his territory.

'I think we must have startled him,' whispered our guide.

I was acutely aware of the double click of the rifle bolt working a round into the breech. Thankfully, there was no need for the scout's old Mannlicher. I watched the lion's rolling mane and the supple lines of muscle along his back as he trotted away, and, for the second time that day, I was alive to the fact that I'd arrived in a truly timeless world.

The South Luangwa Park in Zambia is outstanding for game viewing. The downside is its popularity, which has resulted in the park becoming overcrowded by tourists. The best idea is to get as far upriver as you can, preferably as far as the North Luangwa Park, where, if you're lucky, you won't catch sight of another soul. The game in the north park was decimated by poachers in the 1970s, but it's slowly making a comeback following various anti-poaching initiatives. You have to get out on foot and search far and wide, because the game is still shy. We were rewarded with memorable, close encounters with elephant, buffalo and lion. Sometimes a little too close. Our guide was a mine of information concerning the flora and fauna, including many a wonderful tale to accentuate the capricious nature of Africa. As the sun dipped below the treetops, I loved listening to his stories. The following is one of my own, inspired by this trip.

~

JACK WALSH KEEPS a measured distance between himself and Job, eyeing the bolt-action rifle balanced over the scout's shoulder, reflecting on whether he can trust his life to a relic he imagines has been dragged from a trench at the Somme. Earlier, when the weapon had been laid on the table in camp, he'd run his finger over the five notches sliced crudely into the stock, wanting to believe they might have been poachers who'd crossed the scout's path. One notch – one life; that's what he presumes they signify; except he can't quite bring himself to ask. If he's right, at least it confirms this weapon had once worked. Even if it explodes, Jack reasons, it might provide a suitable distraction in a moment of crisis.

It is, however, just this element of uncertainty that sets his heart racing. The very reason he is in Africa, in this valley they call The Kingdom of the Elephant, is to nourish his yearning for adventure.

'We'll head in the direction of those circling vultures,' Gordon Lockhart says, his words barely audible above the swish of their legs parting the grasses. 'My guess is they're above a kill. We can pick up any predators' tracks and follow them.'

'Sounds good to me,' Jack replies, always appreciating the matter-of-fact manner in which Gordon articulates his intentions.

Jack draws back his shoulders, marvelling at how it might feel to track a predator, to get up close to a dangerous animal. He likes to stride out with such men as these. To be in step with their world.

Shortly, they reach another section of the river. They follow the course of the parched riverbed silently, save for the soft crunch of pebbles beneath their boots. Jack puts up his hand to block the sunlight from his eyes. The vultures hunched on the high branches are clearer now, their naked necks and hooked beaks more defined. They ripple in the haze, sealing the earth from the sky.

The three men scrabble up the crumbling riverbank and once again enter the tall grasses of the floodplain. In places, they reach up to Jack's chest, depositing a fine dust on the front of his cotton shirt. The grasses smell sweet, reminding him of the summer meadows near his home in Sussex. He lightly brushes the dust from the camera lens. When the moment arrives, he doesn't need the dust spoiling his trophy picture. Back in the poky office in Hastings, his work colleagues had been awed when Jack announced where he was going. They'd called him the Great White Hunter. He'd appreciated that, basking in the renown of an adventurer. He's already bagged a photograph of himself holding the rifle. He fancies it will go very well in a plain, wooden frame on his office desk. Now they're closer to the trees, Job slows. He crouches forward, the rifle held low. Jack emulates him, his feet carefully easing a passage through the grass stems.

He keeps his distance, gasping shallow breaths. Ahead of him, Job stops. The scout's left hand rises, his index finger pointing. For the moment, the scout's features are suspended in rigid concentration. Jack is drawn to the man's silently moving lips.

What has he seen?

He follows the line of the African's finger, squinting into the glare, enjoying the throb of blood in his neck. And the giddiness. Yes! In this sudden sensation, he receives true confirmation of why he has come – not entirely to appreciate Africa's immense beauty, its darkness and savagery – but to confront himself. To glimpse something of his soul.

The scout half turns, a flicker of his hand gesturing for Jack to move closer. He grips the camera in both hands, easing forward, sensing Gordon match his every step. On the back of Job's green overalls is a dark stain. An inverted T. Jack fixes his gaze upon it, wondering if Job is scared. Ultimately, it is he who must face the lion.

The thrum filling Jack's ears is the beat of his heart. Yet, he is not afraid. 'Lions,' Gordon breathes close to his ear.

The realisation is like a dagger slicing into his core. He flicks his head from side to side, scouring the sea of grasses. The snatched air burns his lungs.

Where?

Where are the lions, he wants to ask? Only, his lips won't form the question. Jack jumps when Gordon lays a soft hand on his shoulder. He shrugs in an attempt to cover his involuntary reaction. I'm not scared, a voice repeats in his head. Most definitely not scared.

The hand on his shoulder pushes him gently forward. Job is ahead of them by several paces now, and Jack lifts a foot to follow, scuffing the ground with the toe of his boot and stumbling. Jack has a compelling urge to rush forward, yet the hand on his shoulder restrains him. Does Gordon feel his fear?

Job halts abruptly. He jabs the air with his finger, ahead of them and to the left. Jack sees the tops of the tall grasses parting, bending in the wake of an invisible presence. There is no breeze. No sound. Nothing to be seen.

The three men cluster together.

Then, what they've come looking for shows itself above the grasses. The tops of the ears first. Then the crown. Followed by the bloodied muzzle. All of a sudden, the lioness is here, no cage or glass between them, her presence overwhelming. Jack blinks, rooted, as if the grass stalks entangle his legs. Cast under the spell of this creature's amber eyes – in turn, vivid and menacing – Jack is paralysed. His throat constricts as if squeezed by a giant hand.

Gordon whispers for him not to move, and for the briefest of moments, somewhere in the fog of his mind, Jack asks himself whether the scout knew what challenges he faced when he set out today. Yet he came anyway. Because this is how he feeds his family.

Before them, the lioness's bloodied muzzle parts and a deep roar resonates from her, a seismic rumble rolling toward them. Jack staggers backwards, the sound flooding him completely, filling the cavities between bone and sinew, echoing in his head long after the roar has ceased to be heard. The fingers at Jack's shoulder tighten.

'Step backwards, Jack. Very slowly.'

It takes all of his will to move. His legs are wooden. Unresponsive.

The lioness drops from sight. The grasses sway. Gordon points, and the scout nods in response. The scout holds his position while Gordon leads Jack a few paces back. After a while, Job follows after them, never turning, only placing one foot behind him, followed by the other, the rifle hovering close to his shoulder.

Jack notices the stain on the scout's green overalls has spread and is no longer the shape of an inverted T. He can't explain why such a trivial observation so occupies his mind. There's more rustling in the grasses to their left, and Jack refuses to be drawn by the sound. He decides it's the shape of a pear, the stain on the scout's overalls.

'Don't worry. They won't harm us,' Gordon says, the words like a balm to Jack's ears.

As they retreat to the riverbank, Jack feels the tremor begin to work through his body. The muscles in his legs quiver, and he clenches his fists tightly by his sides to subdue the shake.

'You did well. People have been known to run from such an encounter.' Gordon is talking excitedly, hands resting on his hips. To Jack, the voice could be miles away. 'Then it can get pretty hairy,' Gordon is saying.

Job returns to their side, and Gordon pats him on the back. 'Well done, man,' he says. 'That was a bit close.' They return the way they came, the two men dropping down the riverbank together, Jack following on their boot heels. After climbing the opposite bank, they slump down to rest, and Jack hugs his quivering legs to his chest. He looks at where they've come from, seeing the vultures hunched in the tree-tops. Killing time.

'How could you be so sure the lions wouldn't charge?' he asks. 'Experience, I suppose.' Gordon puts the binoculars to his face and glasses the far side of the river. 'Anyway, I let the lioness know we meant her no harm. I gave her a signal, and so she let me know she wouldn't charge us.' Jack runs a hand over his beaded brow. He's not yet ready for Gordon's humour, for he's discovered something of himself that's unsettled him. 'I don't mind telling you, I was damn scared.' There, it was out before he could stop himself.

Gordon chuckles. 'That makes two of us, my friend. And him.' He throws a hand in the direction of Job, who twirls a stalk of grass in his teeth. 'No matter what he might say.'

Jack rubs vigorously at the toe of his boot. It makes him marginally happier to hear this, yet he finds it difficult to look Gordon in the eye. Instead, he inspects the dirt on his thumb. 'What happens if you run?' he can't help asking.

'All sorts can happen.' Gordon lies back on his elbows. 'Isn't that right, Job? And some strange things, besides.'

'Tell me,' Jack says. For a second, Gordon appears to collect his thoughts. 'Perhaps I should tell you the story of a hunter who once roamed the plains and forests of Africa. From childhood, this fellow had learnt the ways of the bush and about all the animals that lived there. He'd learnt to love them. To respect them. And he'd also learnt to hunt them and to understand their mood. He loved his life in the bush. He knew, when he grew up, he would be a hunter like his father.

'Then, much later, when he left college, he set up his own safari outfit. He attracted many clients and enjoyed a well-earned reputation. From the start, he made it a personal rule to maintain a very high discipline with his clients, who often didn't share his regard for the game and the environment in which they lived. After some years, the job he was doing began to grip his conscience and wring it like an old rag, for he was making a lot of money from the people who came to kill the animals he loved so much. Often, after the hunt, a betrayal hung over him like a black cloud, and he began to question why he took these people into his world: people who came with such destruction and vanity in their hearts and who were blind to all else. In time, he began to wonder if they were indeed a mirror of his own existence, a reflection of his own being, and he began to question what he might have become.

'One day, everything changed for him. He followed his client through thick bush, pursuing a lioness from where they'd spotted her on open ground, his client keen to bag it for nothing more than the trophy it rewarded him and the stories he could tell. They continued following her into thick bush, into an environment the hunter knew carried great risk for them. And all the while, the hunter set aside his good judgment, because the client paid extremely well. When the lioness crouched before them, with her teeth bared and her fierce growl, the client lost his nerve and dropped the rifle.

'The hunter took his place, levelling his gun at the lioness. Only then did he see her two small cubs, the cubs she was only wishing to protect, and who were the reason for her existence. He knew for certain she would protect them with her life, and the hunter checked his actions when he saw the spirit in the eyes of that lioness. At that very moment, he experienced the manifestation of all his misgivings, his duplicity and his betrayal. He lowered the rifle, placing his trust in the lioness to allow him to walk free, for he realised he was no longer able to kill a creature of such conviction. And he knew, by such action, he may be saved, or he may not.' Gordon draws up his long legs and rests his arms on his knees. 'The gun bearer, tracker and the client fled to camp, for they no longer had a weapon with which to protect themselves. As they fled, the tracker looked back to see the hunter lower his rifle. Then he saw the lioness pounce. He saw them both fall, lost to the thick bush, and the sight made him hasten to camp, where they gathered what weapons they could, but the tracker held little hope of finding the hunter alive.

'They left camp and, on the way, met the hunter coming towards them down the track. His shirt was torn, and his back bloodied, but he was alive, and he carried his unfired gun in his hand. The tracker rushed to him, asking why he did not kill the lioness. The hunter replied that he'd made a pact with the lioness to set him free and that if she agreed, he would never shoot lions again. Nor would he shoot any of the other animals in the bush or take others to shoot them. On that basis, he told the tracker, the lioness had set him free and, in setting him free, she had also agreed that lions would never attack him. So, he said, a truce had been struck.

'When the hunter had finished telling them this story, he passed his rifle to the gun bearer, as if it was a shackle that fell from his wrists. He walked into camp to clean his wounds, and from that day on, he never hunted again.'

Jack breaks into a smile. 'That's a good story,' he says.

'Yes. It's quite a story.'

THREE DAYS LATER, and Jack is settled in the deep armchair, a gin and tonic on the table by his side. He scrolls through the memory of his digital camera, enjoying the photos he's collected so far on his safari. He's looking forward to transferring them to the bigger screen of his computer. That way he will appreciate them better. Finally, he gets to the photo of himself posing with Job's rifle held across his chest. He considers it for some time while taking a drink from his glass, the tonic fizzing against the roof of his mouth. He likes this photo a lot. Yet he's troubled by the fact it is not really who he is. The man in the picture holding the rifle is an impostor. After some deliberation, he clicks the button to the left and presses DELETE. The image vanishes from the screen.

'Hello, Jack. I didn't see you sitting there so quietly.'

Jack looks up to see Bob Hartley, the camp manager, walk into the mess tent. 'I was checking my library of photos before lunch,' Jack tells him.

'Chris said you'd been up to the north park – to the Kingdom of the Elephant. How was it up there?'

'Wonderful. Another world. Plenty of lions.'

'There are plenty of lions up there.' Bob chuckles as he lifts off his bush hat and tosses it on the sofa. 'Did you go with David?' 'Gordon.' 'Ah. Gordon. And did he show you his scars?'

Jack studies the amused expression on Bob's face. 'What scars?' he asks. 'Gordon used to be a hunter. The story goes he once went with his client after a lioness into thick bush. The client lost his nerve. Ran off, leaving Gordon to deal with her. Gordon wouldn't shoot because she had cubs. Says he made some crazy pact with her. We all reckon he just tasted bad. She bit him and spat him out.' Bob chuckles and pours himself a glass of water from the jug. 'Oh no. Lions don't go near Gordon anymore.'

3

THE JEBEL SARHRO ROCK

2000

I like that Africa features in the name of this motorcycle – Honda Africa Twin. Very appropriate, considering where I'm going. Not much of a challenge for the salesman I bought it from, though. As I look at it now, resting on its stand outside the garage, it's loaded like an overburdened pack-mule. I've lost count of how many times I've packed and unpacked the panniers in my effort to minimise what I take. For days, equipment has been strewn across the floor in the spare bedroom. I'm leaving a lot behind. I hop aboard, squeezing between the luggage and the fuel tank. The bike feels heavy, and I still can't quite believe I intend to ride this machine from the north of England all the way to the wilds of the Jebel Sarhro, a range of mountains in southern Morocco, completely alone.

Adventure, here I come.

I slip the clutch, accelerating up the street. I'm heading for a ferry departing from Plymouth, oblivious to the first major challenge looming over the immediate horizon.

. . .

THE NEXT MORNING, I leave the hotel early for Plymouth docks, no more than a thirty-minute ride away. The plan is for the ferry to transport me across the Bay of Biscay, to Santander, northern Spain, avoiding the arduous ride along France's motorway system. Following a two-day blast through Spain, I'll be at the ferry port of Algeciras, where the short crossing will land me in Ceuta, North Africa. And then it gets serious. Africa! I'm abuzz with excitement as I navigate the streets of central Plymouth. In my mind's eye, I'm already in the Dark Continent – cruising south, the sun in my eyes. I've been doing this for weeks, dreaming of motoring over a desert plain, my dust trail twisting high into the sky.

Down on the docks, a human snake trails from the terminal. I don't like the look of it. Quite possibly the clue lies in the crying kids and bickering adults. A rumour crackles down the line like a lit fuse. If the rumour's true, it's a setback of worrying proportions – and I'm still in England. I shuffle forward in the queue, smouldering quietly. I can't allow myself to believe what I'm hearing. Finally, the harassed assistant is in front of me. A crankshaft in one of the ferry's main engines has broken. My next chance of a crossing to Spain will be in two weeks.

I don't need to hear this. Not after all the planning. The anticipation. I see the corners of the assistant's mouth flicker upward and sense a sliver of hope. I can go to northern France, she declares, though what she's offering is no olive branch. France is crippled by a fuel strike, with 90 per cent of its service stations reportedly closed. I storm from the building. Outside, I pace three circuits of the bike while deliberating what to do. And then I do the same in reverse. I'm not giving in. I'm not going home.

But what's to be done? There's only one acceptable option.

At the nearest service station, I squeeze every last drop of petrol I can into the bike – the spare fuel container, too (an extra five litres). The litre bottle for the stove is also pressed full. It will take me about two hundred and fifty miles before needing more fuel. Perhaps further, if I take it easy. On the newspaper rack, next to the cashier, the front pages speculate over how France's fuel strike will grind the country to a standstill.

By late afternoon I'm on a ferry to Roscoff. It's starting to drizzle.

When I next look at my watch, the time is 23:00 hours, and I'm riding off the ferry and into the town of Roscoff. The rain is still falling, and my visor is beaded with moisture.

I am going to Africa, I tell myself for the umpteenth time, opening the throttle and heading into the whirling mist.

Somewhere near Niort, the digital readout on the dash indicates 03:00 hours. For the moment, I'm diverted off the motorway. I can smell baking bread and the damp earth. I take fuel at every opportunity, as few service stations are open. The roads are mercifully quiet, but then they would be at this ungodly hour. As the road unwinds, I worry about running out of fuel, of becoming stranded for days in a service station, of having to survive on crusty baguette, garlic sausage and, if I'm lucky, a morsel of Brie. I agonise over whether I can mend a puncture as I recall my previous fumbled attempts. And what if I'm to suffer a mechanical breakdown in the middle of the Jebel Sarhro? My mind is awash with worthless speculation. It's quite obviously the witching hour.

Dawn breaks, revealing a clear sky ahead. Not far to Spain now. In the queue at passport control I forget to kick the stand out and, as a consequence, drop the bike on the road. Half the luggage has to be unloaded before I can attempt lifting it upright.

Hallelujah! It's 15:00 hours, and I'm approaching Burgos, in northern Spain. I've been seventeen hours in the saddle and have covered seven hundred and fifty miles since leaving the ferry in Roscoff. I'm just about back on schedule and rather pleased with myself. I think I'll have a San Miguel to celebrate. I swagger into a motel like John Wayne, feeling curiously naked without a helmet on my head. I shower and shovel down some much-needed food. The bed is wonderful. It's so good to lie straight. The falling sun is shining through the curtains, and I drift off to a distant land.

TODAY, a leisurely six-hour ride carries me to Ubeda, a town lying on the plains above Granada. After checking into the Parador, I stroll around the old town of Ubeda, finally settling for a beer at the bar opposite the hotel. Paco is the barman. It's quiet, and we make small talk for a while. He tells me he wants to leave Spain.

'No estoy contento aqui,' he grumbles. 'Estoy un herrador!'

I scratch my chin. *Herrador*? I should remember this word. To help me understand, Paco crouches forward, his right hand making a hammering motion at a point just above his knees. He whinnies loudly.

Ah, yes. He's a farrier. The leathery-skinned old man at

the next table breaks into a toothless grin at our antics. The dog at his feet gives a big, pink yawn. I wish Paco the best of luck and retire to the hotel.

THE INFAMOUS N340 road between Malaga and Algeciras is busy. It's dubbed The Highway of Death for its frequent high-speed crashes. As I pass Marbella, the abundant traffic shuffles at a pace barely capable of crushing a gnat. Waves of heat radiate from the tarmac as I weave slowly between the cars. There's no chance of a high-speed crash today.

After five hours, I reach Algeciras and board the next ferry for Ceuta. Taking no chances, I rope the bike against a sturdy pipe, even though the sea is flat calm. On deck, I appreciate the cool breeze as I watch the Rif Mountains loom. Africa inches closer. The pulse quickens.

Ceuta is the curious melting pot I remember – a border town where the last vestiges of European culture are overwhelmed by the exotic Maghreb. I find the hotel I'm looking for in the central square, another Parador, and quickly settle in its remnants of Western society that seem so out of place. Before turning in for the night, I set the alarm so as to arrive early at the border, though quite frankly, I shouldn't have bothered.

I SWEEP up to the Spanish–Morocco border before dawn. My game plan is to outwit the rabble. I cross that invisible line marking Spain's tenuous grip on a blob of North Africa and come to a ramshackle collection of buildings. There's an orange glow from the single street light. The place is deserted, save for two unshaven policemen huddled together.

'Immigration,' they grunt simultaneously, dispatching me to a building with a lot of darkened windows. I go there, sticking my nose against the pane of glass. In the gloom, I make out a man lying on the floor beside a chair. His feet disappear beneath a table. A tie hangs from the chair.

This must be the immigration officer, I presume. Fast asleep. But what to do?

I raise a hand, about to tap on the window, when a snore rips through the silence. One eyelid flicks open accusingly, as if it was I who'd made such a commotion. Yet it's a fleeting contact, for he rolls onto his other side, shifts his legs and instantly falls quite still.

I step back, feeling the initiative slipping. It's by now quite clear why I'm the only one attempting to cross this border. I slump down on the step, gripping a fist-load of documents.

Some hours later, and I'm on the road to Tetouan, among multi-coloured plastic bags pirouetting along the roadside like tumbleweed. Further still, a woolly-haired man, trousers round his ankles, squats in the grasses at the roadside. Soon enough, tin-shack accommodation indicates the beginnings of suburbia. Already, I've negotiated several check-points – police, customs, immigration. I have the awful feeling the border was only a dry run for what's to come.

In the centre of Tetouan, from every nook and cranny weep hustlers and marijuana peddlers. I suck them in, as if I'm the plughole in an enormous sink. Hounds hunt with less fervour than this crowd. Even when I open the throttle and jump a red light or two, there are still three hustlers on a scooter cruising a little too close to me. I charge up the hill leading out of town and finally lose them in the mist. The scooter is no match against the Honda's lumpy 750.

I pass the turning to Chefchaouen, coming to a fork in the road. The sign has gone, but I'm pretty sure I should turn left. Two young men emerge at the roadside, slumped shoulder to shoulder. I look from my map into their glassy eyes. The imbecilic grins are the final clue to their befuddled state. They say I should take them on the motorbike to Ketama.

'It's a beautiful journey,' the guy with the beard promises.

'It's FREEDOM!' the other enthuses.

Ketama is the heartland of Morocco's marijuana production. I've been there before, some years ago, and will not be hurrying back. I tell them I'm following the road beyond Meknes.

The bearded one rises like a marionette. 'Then may Allah be with you,' he says.

I say thank you for the good wishes, at the same time hoping I won't need him.

It's mid-afternoon, and I'm on a road leading over a bleak and parched desert plateau above Azrou. After seven hours on the road, I pull into the car park of a sprawling hotel. There is a large swimming pool with dead leaves bobbing on the surface. Inside the building, the corridors are long and eerily quiet. At dinner, the dining room remains deserted. The waiter who serves me is the same generously proportioned fellow who gave me the room key when I checked in. I imagine he's the chef, too. The waiter-chef-receptionist observes me from the doorway to the kitchen while I eat. I have the strong impression I'm the only guest in the hotel. Suddenly consumed by loneliness, I'm shot through with a feeling of how I'm the last person left in the whole world... except for this multi-faceted waiter.

Later, after retiring to my room, cackles of laughter

intrude on the monastic silence. Somewhere, a door slams. The cackle is extinguished. Through the open window, the breeze carries the muted bleating of goats from the plain to the north, and the occasional call of the herdsman. The curtain dances to the tune of the breeze. There are footsteps in the corridor, stopping briefly outside my door. Whispered voices drift through the crack beneath it. The footsteps move on. I reach down from my bed to check the parachute distress flare is where I left it. The first one through this door gets thirty-thousand candelas of rocket in the gut.

'Sweet dreams,' I murmur, soon drifting off to sleep.

FROM AZROU, I make a diversion through the Foret de Cedres. The pine and cedar forests and the lakes are an odd contrast to yesterday's desert landscape. I swerve to avoid a troop of monkeys, and they scatter into the trees.

At El-Ksiba, on the road to Marrakech, I head south, to the Lake Plateau. The road twists through oak woods, much as I remember it, only now the tarmac penetrates further into the Atlas Mountains. Eventually, it gives way to a dirt track following the course of the river in the valley bottom. The water is low, and fresh motorbike tracks have cut through the dirt. I buy fruit from some kids along the way.

I stop for lunch by the river – a tin of sardines and the fruit I've just bought. All is peace and quiet, only the burble of the river, until a couple of youths materialise from nowhere and settle on the ground opposite me.

'Two motorbikes came through not long ago,' they say.

'Where are they from?' I ask. They shake their heads, and we very quickly exhaust our collection of common words and simply stare at each other. I give them a tin of sardines and get on my way.

The dirt switchback takes me up to the Lake Plateau. I coast down to the edge of Lake Tislit and walk among the trees where I'd made camp before, with JP, Pete, Wandy and Rolf. That was twelve years ago now. The sky is grey and the lake inky black. A cool wind blows off the purple hills. It bends the grasses and ripples the surface of the lake. I try to draw on those good memories. Not much has changed here except what I feel for this place. Its barrenness. The solitude. I had planned on camping under the trees and chasing the past. But there is nothing to keep me here now. I kick at the light soil littered with cigarette butts and move on.

After Imilchil, the narrow road twists and turns through the valleys. I haven't seen another traveller for hours when two motorcyclists appear round the next bend. The tracks I've been following must have been theirs. One of them holds a map between outstretched arms. A couple of shepherd boys stand next to them. Stopping beside them to exchange news of the road, I discover they are German. For a moment, I admire their bikes brimming with boxes and all manner of equipment. I'm sure half of Bavaria is bolted to their machines. In truth, a van might have better suited their purpose.

'Gorge du Todra?' one of them demands, his face burnt puce by the sun, flakes of skin peeling from his forehead. It seems I point ahead a little too confidently, for they readily agree to follow the clever Englander. The map is folded neatly away, but remounting their bikes is not so straightforward. Considerable hopping is involved. One of them catches the heel of his boot in the fleece draped over the seat, and is forced to begin all over again.

Not much later, and dusk is upon us. The road is never-ending, twisting and turning as we descend from the hills.

We should have arrived at the gorge by now. I'm beginning to think I've gone wrong somewhere along the way.

Some hours later, the beam of my headlights cut through the darkness. Ahead of us shine the lights from a collection of buildings. The tarmac road peters out. Dust rises thickly from the wheels, and my headlights illuminate two characters sitting on a rock. I've clocked up twelve hours in the saddle today, and I'm tired and aggravated, and I suspect the 'clever' Englander is about to eat an enormous chunk of humble pie.

The dust is thick in my mouth as I take out the map to locate our position. The Germans dismount and smoke a cigarette each. One of them illuminates the torch attached to his forehead. He plods around exhaling smoke, looking much like a locomotive that's run off the rails. There's nowhere to stay here in Rich, the two characters on the rock tell us. We take their advice and head for Errachidia. It's another sixty kilometres I really don't need today.

The shapes and lights of Errachidia rise out of the blackness. As we close in on the town, the bike coughs twice and stalls. I'm out of fuel. I coast to a halt at the roundabout, my boots crunching the sand coating the road. Traffic weaves around me as I refill the tank from the spare container. A youth lingers next to me, ash from his cigarette tumbling perilously close to the fuel. His name is Mahfoud. I ask if he knows of a campsite close by.

'Why don't you stay here?' He points behind a thick hedge adjacent to the roundabout.

'A proper campsite,' I tell him.

'It's way out of town. But my uncle has a hotel.'

I give him a long, hard look, weighing up this gem of information. 'D'you speak German?'

'Oh, yes!'

'Then go and tell those two.'

The other two motorcyclists have agreed to follow, and Mahfoud hops aboard my bike, juggling various bits of luggage to make room for himself. The uncle's hotel is simply appalling. The bed is a filthy mattress pushed against a wall smeared with dirt. I know the toilet is at the end of the corridor because the stench is already crawling all over me.

Back outside in the street, a drunk is shouting at us like a madman. We tell Mahfoud to take us to another hotel, which turns out to be slightly less appalling. It's down a narrow street that might as well be called Muggers Alley. Sand lies thickly on the street – all the better for soaking up the blood, I muse. Right now, I'm glad of the Germans' company, and we finally introduce ourselves. Their names are Klaus and Steiner.

We stick the bikes in a lockup and pray they'll still be there in the morning.

It's 22:00 hours, and Mahfoud is taking us to a restaurant he knows. The town is deserted, as is the restaurant. It turns out Klaus has an unusual taste in après-bike wear. The legs of his leather trousers are laced together with thongs, causing him to creak with each step. He sounds like a rusty hinge advancing down the street. A wood-handled dagger pokes from the right boot.

In the restaurant, we share a dish containing a small rubbery carcass and a selection of vegetables. 'What is this thing?' I ask, poking it with my knife.

'It's a chicken,' replies Mahfoud.

Klaus shakes his head. Regardless of how many times he repeats the same word, I'm still not going to understand him. Neither does Mahfoud. The German creaks as he takes an electronic translator from his trouser pocket. He stabs the keys and turns it to me. SPARROW, it reads. I consider proposing an alternative but fear that, by the time I'm finished typing, whatever it is on this plate will have been eaten.

Mahfoud turns out to be the local entrepreneur – beer, wine, cigarettes, fine women, marijuana. Anything goes, here in Errachidia. He even owns a camel capable of transporting us deep into the Sahara Desert.

'The camel is called Jimi Hendrix,' he shrills, strumming a pretend guitar and making an odd jigging motion. 'Jimi, he flies over the dunes!'

'Ve go mit moto!' Klaus grumbles, sounding much like his motorbike on tick-over.

Mahfoud barely draws breath – the latest GPS navigation can be ours by morning, he promises.

Klaus's hand hovers dangerously near the knife in his right boot. 'Kein GPS!' he snarls, his face a patchwork of loose skin and glowing scabs. 'Ich habe ein Kompass.'

I eye the German warily. At least there will be an audible warning if he lunges for his knife.

Back in the hotel, I lay out the sleeping bag on the bed. I reckon it's safer than unleashing what could be between these sheets. I don't bother undressing. I take a leaf from Klaus's book and keep my Winchester hunting knife within arm's reach. My stomach rumbles with hunger.

WE RECOVER our bikes from the lockup early the next morning and repack our gear. Children gather to watch the strange men pressing buttons on a little plastic box and passing it back and forth. We communicate by employing very short words. The children are giggling. Klaus and Steiner are going to Erg Chebbi and along the Algerian border. I tell them to watch out for Jimi the camel. As I leave, Klaus is taking a fix with his compass and glowering at the sun. Sweat beads his forehead.

I hit the tarmac road toward Ouarzazate, a black, shimmering line carving through the sand, and open up the twin.

After three hours, I reach Tinerhir and take a room in a castellated hotel, staying the night in one of its turrets. In the dining room, the chef presents me with the most enormous couscous. It's very delicious and very welcome, considering last night's meagre offering. Later (much later), I waddle to my room.

NARROW SHAFTS of sunlight strike through the shutters. A cockerel is crowing. A dog howls. The bathroom occupies the corner of the room, partitioned from the bedroom by a thin wall. The bathroom floor is of bare concrete, and a hole in the middle doubles as the toilet and the plughole. Directly above the hole hangs the shower head. I stand at the entrance, gawping from one to the other – hole to shower to hole – experiencing a moment of indecision.

Today, I cross the Jebel Sarhro. It's a wild, nomadic country, a place where the great warriors of the south, the Ait Atta, made their last and bloody stand against the French on Jebel Bou Gafer in 1933.

On turning south, the tarmac road soon ends, and a gravel plain opens out before me. The horizon shimmers, a misty beige, and far-away peaks rise above the haze. I stop to take it in. I've experienced this scene before. In my dreams, I've been here. The sun's heat presses around me, relentless, stealing my vigour. It's frightening how quickly it achieves this. The breath rasps my parched throat. The only way to stay cool is to accelerate into this furnace, stones thrashing against the underside of the engine, the machine juddering on the corrugations, a fine dust settling over my clothes. I'm laughing. Adventure motorcycling doesn't get much better than this. I stand up on the pegs, playing the bike's movement through my hands and my legs, easing the needle beyond sixty mph.

The landscape unfurls, undulating gently.

I pass a crumbling fortification on a low hill.

A mirage floats in the distance – I chase it until it's lost at the foot of the mountains. Behind me, the dust trail snakes into the sky.

I suffer a tricky moment in deep sand, the machine wanting to go every which way but straight ahead. My heart thumps in my throat as I ride it out. This is not the time to crash. Not out here.

The track climbs for some time, entering a land of deep ravines, distorted volcanic pinnacles and flat-topped mesas. I have a GPS attached to the bars, but don't need it. I ask a goat herder if I'm on the right track to Nekob. It seems I am.

Now I'm in a valley, among almond groves and lush date palms. Children crowd me, their hands overflowing with fruit. I stop and buy some.

Beyond the valley, I cross a high plain. Huge, grey rock formations rise above the surrounding hills like the vertebrae of enormous dinosaurs.

The track narrows and ruts as it rises steeply, the sheer sides tumbling into the ravine. The machine doesn't want to go up. It slips in and out of the ruts, and the rear wheel skitters as it negotiates the rocks. My legs paddle furiously either side on the steeper sections, the luggage panniers constantly cracking my ankles. I know the bike just wants to lie down and give up. I won't let it for the simple reason I might not get it upright again. I fight it and talk to it in equal measure, coaxing it up the hill like an obstinate mule. It's become such a numb weight, this machine.

Later, with my arms and legs burning from the effort of reaching yet another false summit, I stand beside the motorcycle, gulping down water and soaking up the view. This cooler breeze is a sweet relief, and I gaze about me in the silence – these arid mountains are all mine.

'Salaam!'

My heart leaps, and I spin to face the voice behind me. A girl has crept up on me. Her face is nut-brown, cheeks ruddy, a blue scarf tied about her head.

How do they do that, this trick of appearing from nowhere?

The girl climbs down from the rocks above. Her pink jumper has a pattern of red roses in a band across the chest. She comes toward me, her hand outstretched, the fist clenched. When she opens her fingers, there is a small, jagged rock in the palm of her hand. I take it from her. It is ochre and black, and the sun glints from minute crystals. I weigh it in my palm. I've had a bellyful of these rocks. It's no different to the ones I've been toiling over for the past hour. In fact, I hate these rocks.

'Cinq dirham,' she suggests.

I glare at her. She has to be kidding – I haven't even recovered my breath. With the toe of my boot, I shovel together the very same ochre and black rocks whose minute crystals glint in the sun. I quickly have a small mound. She gets the gist of it.

'Quatre dirham,' she offers.

Her olive eyes enchant me. They give nothing away. Her jaw is fixed, and the soundlessness settles between us as I close my fingers over the rock. If I hadn't stopped to catch my breath, this girl would have missed her opportunity.

Serendipity. And yet. Who in their right mind buys a piece of rock on a mountain?

I shake my head, digging the four dirhams from my pocket. I give her the money, placing the Jebel Sarhro rock inside the map case strapped on top of the fuel tank.

Satisfied with the trade, the girl retreats to a rock, from where she sits and watches. I wonder how long she must wait for the next person to fall for her curious charm.

I reach the final summit by mid-afternoon and make a brew of tea while absorbing the landscape. The sun is warm on my face as I sit on the slab above a gorge. It is incredibly peaceful here. I expect someone to materialise from the surrounding cover at any moment, except this time, I am entirely alone. There is nobody but me, and I relish the wind blowing through my soul, a temporary deliverance from life's distractions. I shall enjoy the sensation for as long as I can hold it.

Down on the lower plains, the wind has strengthened, whipping up a sandstorm. A man looms from out of the haze. I haven't seen a settlement in a long time and stop to give him a bottle of water to take on his way. He's going home, he tells me, soon vanishing into the haze.

I reach Nekob and follow the blacktop to Ouarzazate.

It's been another twelve-hour day in the saddle, and I consider I've earned somewhere decent to stay. In Ouarzazate, I park outside a hotel resembling a sultan's palace in all its grandeur. The interior of the property reveals a world of cool marble and intricate Moorish architecture. Checking over my shoulder, a trail of Jebel Sarhro dust marks my passage to the reception desk. I ask if they have a room. The man in the starched white jacket and gold braid looks me up and down. His eyes follow the trail of dirt from the toe of my scuffed boots all the way back to the door, which, I can tell, is exactly where he would like to see me go. I already know the answer. Outside, I cause a small sandstorm when I brush the rest of the dust from my clothing. I have to concede the receptionist has a point.

I find a place with expedition vehicles parked outside. This looks more suited to my appearance. On my way to the lobby, I savour the emergence of a vast pool, where a palm tree grows from an island in the middle. This is more my kind of place.

The pool is wonderfully refreshing. And so is the beer.

THE NEXT DAY, the pool remains wonderfully refreshing. As does the beer. I stay for another day's R&R.

Lying in the shade on this sunbed, I have a moment when my conscience niggles. The motorbike is loaded with camping gear that hasn't yet seen the light of day. Never mind: 'Monsieur. Another beer, please.'

OUTSIDE THE FRONT of the hotel, I strap my bag to the seat and make a quick check of the machine. The unofficial guardian appears at my side from beneath the palms. He says he's been here all night. I suspect he's here every night, going by the scalloped earth at the base of the tree. I give him some coins, a box of Uncle Ben's long grain rice and my last two tins of sardines in tomato sauce. He looks delighted, shaking the box of rice close to his ear and slipping the tins of fish into his pocket. Frankly, I'm glad to see the back of them. A very satisfactory arrangement is concluded.

On the road leaving Ouarzazate, I pass the film studios where Lawrence of Arabia and James Bond have both strutted their stuff. The road sign tells me I'm heading for

Marrakech, where I harbour ideas of exploring the souk and the famous Jemaa El Fnaa. When I finally reach the city, I ease the bike through one of the arches in the ancient walls, where utter chaos is revealed. A surge of frantic humanity blocks the street. This place is way too busy. A donkey, ears back, eyes rolling, bolts past me, disappearing beyond the city walls. Just at that moment, I reckon he's the smartest donkey in the whole world. I turn around and follow him out.

I head south toward the Tizi-n-Test pass and then stop to call the hotel in Ouirgane where I've promised myself a short break. They agree to reserve me a room. I cut the connection, smiling cunningly, because I'm still not looking my best. There's no way they can refuse me entry now that I have a reservation.

The hotel lies in the foothills of the western Atlas. It has a winding drive. When I pull up at the property, I clock the porter hovering by the entrance door, pondering if he should help with my luggage, or simply toss me his spare change. He gives the distinct impression of never having carried quite such a soiled bag. Is it a look of pity or contempt he flashes me? I match his loping gait and wonder how many of their guests turn up from England by motorcycle, via the Jebel Sarhro.

Inside the property, the receptionist visibly shudders. He shoots a look from me to the porter and back again, an expression suggesting that hauling tramps off the street is outside the porter's job description. He starts telling me they're full and then stiffens when realising he's been outmanoeuvred. I feel somewhat ashamed of my duplicity. His manicured fingers clamp my credit card.

The porter leads me from the reception out into the garden. The rooms are little cottages dotted around it. The garden is full of greenery and plants – the very picture of tranquillity. It could be the south of England. Roses are abundant. A group of three drink tea in the shade by the pool. They're speaking English. They stop talking as I approach, sniffing the air with that very British look of disapproval. Birdsong ceases. I feel the whole world has fallen silent, save for the loose heel of my boot, which slaps on the path with each step I take. The silver duct tape holding it together for the past two days has chosen this very moment to unravel itself. It trails, like an ugly streamer, in my wake. The porter snatches a look behind him and quickens his pace.

SLAP! SLAP! SLAP! goes the heel of my boot.

I TAKE a morning ride up to the Tizi-n-Test pass. It's a spectacular, twisting road. Dwellings perch on the mountainside. The pass is at two thousand and ninety-two metres altitude. I stare into the southern haze before returning to Ouirgane. The afternoon is reserved for the pool.

On the television, BBC World 24 tells me the fuel strike will, in all probability, extend further across Europe. It is predicted that Spain will be next. I decide it's time to get moving.

BY EARLY AFTERNOON the next day, I arrive in Rabat and do a circuit of the city. I contemplate stopping for the night, but my heart is not in it. I move on, continuing north, cruising at good speed on the motorway. The light has fallen as I thread through the streets of Tangier. Again, I think about staying, but I'm so tired I can't be doing with the hassle of finding a hotel or dealing with the hustlers in the streets. It's so crazy this town. I just want to get out. I head for the docks, where the chaos continues. I stop outside a travel office, and I'm immediately jumped upon. One of the touts is a little overzealous. He snatches my passport from my hand, though he quickly senses what a very short fuse he's ignited. He immediately gives it back. In a travel office, I part with cash, get my ticket and catch the last ferry out.

AT 02:00 HOURS, the ferry docks at Algeciras port. The Spanish customs officer wants to know what I have to declare. He looks at me blankly when I show him the Jebel Sarhro rock. As I turn it over in my hand, the pinprick-sized crystals flash in the artificial light. It has no value and yet is priceless. Such a souvenir as this cannot be bought in any shop.

Riding into the night, I wonder if she's still up there on her mountain, the girl with the nut-brown face, awaiting the next unsuspecting traveller.

4

THE NATURE OF THE BEAST

There's a wonderful camp in Botswana's Okavango Delta specialising in horseback safaris, a magical way to approach game. To gallop alongside zebra, giraffe and antelope is an experience never to be forgotten. In camp, fine tents are set among the trees, and at night, they are surrounded by the calls of the wildlife. Life in camp is intimate and, at times, intriguing. It's not quite Agatha Christie; you must let your imagination run a little, as I have done in this short story.

~

THE CLINK of glass signals Donald is making cocktails. He does this every night, eyes roving the small gathering, a tight grin on his lips.

Most of us are wise to him now. Marjorie was his latest victim. She's a rather aloof Englishwoman who arrived in camp the previous evening, following a long journey via Johannesburg. Donald's Bloody Mary rendered her a quivering wreck in record time. He'd clapped his hands once in delight when the camp staff carried her off to her tent.

Beyond the campfire, Tony lowers himself into one of the canvas chairs next to Marjorie. 'Are you on the Bloody Mary again tonight, Marj?' he probes, loud enough for all to hear.

'Good heavens! Not tonight. I'm a Virgin Mary tonight.'

'Good show,' he says.

I notice how Tony appears to have recovered much of his sang-froid. Only the soiled shirt bears evidence of the earlier tumble from his horse. He twists in the chair. 'Fix me a gimlet, will you, Don,' he calls toward the bar. 'And I'm sure Bella will have one of those vodka things you do rather well.'

I watch Tony lop one leg over the other, pressing himself deeper into the chair. The firelight reflects off his calf-length boots. I suspect he's polished them since coming in from the ride, which is why I'm surprised he hasn't changed his shirt. He's smoothing the leg of his trousers with long strokes of his palm as he talks. His voice carries above all the others.

Tony and his wife, Arrabella, are from a smart part of London, and they own a large house in the Hampshire countryside. He'd imparted as much the first evening they arrived – to anyone who was prepared to listen, that is. Although going by the tittle-tattle, it seems everyone has by now endured his tiresome tales of corporate vanquish, as if to air them might dispel any notion one may harbour concerning his character. I have to admit, in the past couple of days, I've found him marginally interesting, as a disagreeable person is prone to be. And yet, much like a mountain stream, everything beneath the surface is so apparent.

Donald saunters from the bar with a silver tray in his hands. He does the rounds, dispensing liquid largesse like a mad chemist. When he's finished, he slumps his big frame into the creaking canvas chair next to me, sporting his modest grin. The crimson-coloured scarf is loose at his neck, and there's a wicked twinkle in his eye.

Donald slips from one anecdote to another with the consummate skill of a man who's lived life to the full, and then some. He'd been in the furniture business for many years. That was until he'd hit a particularly difficult period of trading, and the financiers called in the loans. Times had completely changed after that he volunteered one evening. 'Bad, bad times,' Donald emphasised. Even his wife left him, shacking up with her fitness trainer – a Brazilian half her age. Each night, he offers another segment into the mosaic. As we'd been called to dinner the previous evening, he leaned very close, whispering, 'Friends are not always what they might appear.' He'd been staring across the fire when he spoke, to where his lifelong friend Tony had been holding forth with another tale of enrichment.

'People should be wary of you, Donald,' I say, reinforcing the point by sloshing the strong drink in my glass. He rests the silver tray on his lap. 'Nonsense. People only need be wary of themselves.' He takes a long drink from his glass, the tonic fizzing. He swallows. 'I'm merely facilitating their... inclination.'

'Facilitating or influencing?'

His piercing eyes are on me. 'It's the nature of the beast,' he says.

It's almost dark now. I sweep over the human shapes around the fire, their conversation buzzing with the day's sights and experiences, the camaraderie enriched by our African adventure. 'I'll tell you a story about human nature.' Donald leans closer to me. 'Many years ago, there was a boy called David who lived in a hamlet on the edge of an enormous forest. He had a friend called Max, who had been like a brother to him.

'By day, David worked alongside his father in the fields and the forests. He grew up a strong young man, popular for the work he did for his neighbours. Before long, he started courting Laura, and there was talk of how they would be married next summer.' Donald breaks off to slop back a mouthful of gin. He crunches a cube of ice between his teeth before continuing. 'One day, there was uproar. A very rare and valuable piece of jewellery belonging to Freda, a woman so old nobody knew her age, had been stolen. Now, it just so happened that David often helped Freda tend her garden and repair her old house. When the jewellery went missing, David was the first to be suspected. Some said, to better himself before his marriage to Laura.

'The problem for David was, when they searched his bedroom, they found the piece of jewellery. He denied having taken it, but in a hamlet like that, where trust was absolute, it was the worst thing that could possibly have befallen him. He was castigated, driven away to live his days like a hermit in a small hut on the edge of the forest.

'One day, Max visits David in his hut. By then, Max had inherited his father's farm and was a relatively wealthy young man. He'd come to taunt David over his fall from grace, and to tell him how it was he who had taken the jewellery from Freda, and how he had made the villagers believe David was nothing more than a common thief. When he left, David saw the marriage band on Max's finger, and it was a painful reminder of how Max had also stolen Laura.

'From that day, David plotted his revenge. He encouraged Max to visit him and to taunt him, pretending his words did not hurt, when all the while he learnt many things about Max – his vanity, his greed and his ignorance. Finally, David had an idea. He took a rock the size of his fist, and he painted it gold, placing it high up on a shelf in his hut, where the light was not so good. When Max next visited, he saw the golden rock on the shelf and asked David where he had found such a valuable object. "Deep in the forest," David told him. "You must take me," Max demanded, "and we shall share all the riches we find there."

'The following week, Max came again. It was a beautiful morning, the day already hot, and Max arrived with nothing more than the light clothes he wore. David, on the other hand, carried his food, water and a heavy coat, for they were going deep into the forest. They set off, walking all day, until the light above the canopy of trees faded. "We should rest for the night," David told Max. Max again demanded to know where David found the gold. "Maybe another hour from here," David said, pointing ahead through the trees. When David awoke the next day, he was not surprised to discover Max had already left. He knew his greed would get the better of him, and he suspected that Max would most likely become lost on his own in the forest. For somebody inexperienced, the forest was a dangerous place. If chance is not with Max, David thought to himself, I will never have to see him again. And from that day on, nobody ever did.' Donald drains his glass, his lips curled in a look of triumph. 'So, do you think David facilitated Max's demise or influenced it?'

'Perhaps David should choose his friends more carefully.'

'But do you think he should have a conscience for what he did?' 'Max most likely killed himself,' I reply after a moment. 'Exactly my point. Now, if you'll excuse me, I think I'll change for dinner.'

. . .

After dinner, we retire to the canvas chairs surrounding the fire. The flames lick around the wood. A log explodes in a shower of sparks.

'Do you think tomorrow we could look for the pride of lion?' Donald asks, the brandy glass hovering close to his lips.

'On horseback?' Peter, the guide, pushes sand onto the sparks with his boot.

'Why not?' 'No reason not to. If we're careful.' 'Perhaps it should be just a chaps' outing.' Donald winks conspiratorially at Tony. 'I know you fell today, Tony. But you'd be up for it, wouldn't you?' 'Oh, Tony, I'm not sure.' Arrabella pulls the padded jacket closer to her. 'Rubbish! Bella, it was just the bloody horse. Of course, I'm up for it, Don. A good bit of male bonding, hey? And I'd like a fine picture of me with lion.' 'And how about you?' Donald looks at me. 'You'd be up for it, wouldn't you?' 'Oh, yes,' I agree. 'Let's have some adventure.' 'We'll head out at first light. Say six o'clock at the barn?' Peter pushes himself up from the chair. 'I'm going to get some sleep.' Donald slaps his leg, the firelight dancing in his eyes. 'Who's for another drink? Tony, you'll have one, for sure.'

By midmorning the next day, the heat is fierce on our backs. Ahead of us stretches an expanse of grassland, a quivering, honey-coloured sea. In the sea is an island of dense palm scrub. Real fan palms rise loftily from it. The horses loll in its direction.

'We can rest a while in the shadow of those palms,' Peter offers. 'Good idea.' Tony's face is red beneath the broad rim of his hat, the front of his olive shirt black with sweat. He fumbles the water bottle from its pouch on the saddle.

Donald rises in his saddle, scanning the area to our left, where the grasses give way to woodland. Tony's camera dangles from Donald's shoulder. 'Wonder where those damn lions are,' he hisses. We are within twenty yards of the island when Peter's left hand shoots up. We rein in, standing the horses while peering into the shadows thrown by the palm leaves. 'There they are,' Peter breathes. 'There are your lions.' Despite the sticky heat, a chill runs the length of my back. They are lying in the broken shadow. A male lazily raises his head. The sun flashes in his yellow eyes, his mane dark and full. Then, a female raises her head, a little to his right, and then another next to her.

'God! We've absolutely got to get you in this shot, Tony. I have the camera ready.'

Tony kicks back his leather boots, his horse jolting forward. It seems the horse hasn't yet caught the lions' scent.

'Come back, Tony! They've young with them.' Peter's hand rests on the butt of his rifle. 'Wow. This is going to look something on your boardroom wall.' Donald brings up the camera. 'You really look the part, Tony, old boy. Hemingway, eat your heart out.'

Tony straightens his back, pulling in his stomach. The camera whirrs, snapping a series of shots.

'Dr Livingstone, I presume?' Donald whoops. 'These are going to be great photos, Tony.' Tony stands his horse, resting his clenched fist against his thigh. The sunlight flashes off his boots. The camera whirrs again. Behind him, the male lion and the lioness rise to their feet. My horse snorts, ears pricked. 'Tony, get back here,' Peter orders. Tony turns in the saddle. Two lionesses rise from the grass. I hear Peter cuss. Three more lionesses slink into the long grass. They fan out quickly, efficiently, and my heart hammers against my chest when I see their intention. I can barely hold my horse. He's turning, snorting. I slacken the reins and let him go. 'Ride!' Peter shouts. Tony emits a high-pitched squeal and is thrown off balance when his horse bolts. Peter's horse rears and twists. He tugs the rifle free from the scabbard.I thrust the reins forward, digging my heels, hoping for enough lead between myself and the lions. Behind me, I hear Peter's shouts and the pounding hooves of another horse at my side. I snatch a look. It's Donald. I'm sure he's grinning, possibly even laughing, but any sound he makes is drowned by the wind and pounding hooves. The rifle cracks, the report rolling back off the line of dense woodland.

Donald, slightly ahead of me, pulls back on the reins. He rises in the saddle, back arched, forearms taught. I do the same, pulling hard. My horse yields, bucking twice before coming to a restless stop.

Tony charges past us, one hand gripping the horse's mane, the other the saddle. The reins flap uselessly below the animal's outstretched neck as he thumps up and down in the saddle, his face creased in a look bordering extreme discomfort and absolute terror. The rifle cracks again. I swing the horse round, and Donald is by my side. He's wheezing, chest heaving. His horse is frothing, the neck lathered in sweat. I breathe a sigh of relief; Peter's warning shots have caused the lions to retreat. 'That was a bit close,' I say. 'Too bad!' Donald turns in the saddle, in the direction of the pounding hooves. Tony is far away now, almost at the edge of the woodland. 'He's got the luck of the Devil, that one.'

5

THE CROSSING

We found them at dawn. Not far from camp.

The lion was the first to enter the river. Soon, he was swimming, the strong current checking his passage, small eddies emerging in his wake. As he swam, the water broke around his full mane and over his back.

When he reached the far bank, he shook himself, an arc of moisture hanging momentarily in the air. Then he trotted towards the far woodland, where another lion, proud and majestic, emerged from the shade to greet him. They brushed flanks, strolling side by side into the cover.

The others crossed after that, sometimes in pairs, sometimes alone. Each time they reached the far side, the same lion emerged from the shade to greet them. I'd never seen anything quite like that before.

The cub sat on the riverside beside its mother, watching them go. Occasionally, he rose on all fours, anxious to follow, taking a tentative step forward and then sitting again. After a while, he went forward, forging his way between the reeds to gingerly tap at the water. The lioness went and fussed around him. The cub placed each paw cautiously in the water, each time a little deeper. No sooner had he cleared the shallows than the current took him, carrying him down the river. He thrust his head above the surface, thrashed and turned, scrabbling back to the bank, where he shook the water from his body, and they both went and sat some more, mother and cub, watching the river.

A little later, the lioness went forward into the water, and the cub followed her. She stood up to her belly, turned her head to him, and the cub came in next to her. She nudged him and pushed him ahead of her into the flowing water. Then, with her muzzle on his rear, she propelled him forward, until soon her body became submerged. She kicked hard against the current for them both, and in that manner, they drifted down the river, emerging on the opposite side, some distance downstream.

After they'd shaken the water off, the cub trotted after the lioness into the woodland, until they too disappeared.

6

ICE STATION AFRICA

2001

The aeroplane banks left on its final approach, shuddering as it descends. Through the window, I scan the blue ocean, watching the dark blob of the aircraft glide across the waves, the shadow and its form slowly merging. We swoop over the foaming surf and the beach, the willowy palms and the baobab trees. After that, from among the rust-coloured earth and scrub undergrowth, comes a disorderly collection of simple, square dwellings, and a kind of civilization hewed from the Sahel is finally revealed.

I sweep the crumbs from lunch off my trousers and slip the completed immigration form and passport into the breast pocket of my shirt. I can hardly believe I'm finally here. It needed tenacity and a good deal of detective work to track JP down. Not for the first time, I ponder how life in prison might have changed him.

I make a quick exit from the plane, only to be assaulted by the first blast of hot air. Crossing the tarmac, I spy at some distance the Russian-made helicopter, its camouflage paintwork fading, the rotors missing, and the grass gradually entangling the undercarriage. A military Land Rover patrols the airfield perimeter, a soldier in the back clinging to a cradle-mounted machine gun.

Thankfully, the temperature inside the terminal is relatively cool, and I join the excited holidaymakers shuffling into an orderly queue. A man in civilian clothes stands to one side. His white shirt is open at the neck, and a sheet of paper across his chest bears my name in bright red ink. I break from the line and go to him.

'I'm Mr James,' I tell him.

'Welcome to Africa, Mr James.' The man's face transforms from a picture of anxiety to a beaming smile. 'I am Kebba,' he says.

Kebba clasps my hand, making up for the soft, clammy grip with a vigorous shake.

'We came last week looking for you, but you were not on that flight. Mr JP wrote the wrong date in the diary.' He holds out his hand. 'Please, give me your passport. I will fetch a stamp, and then we can go.'

Kebba ushers me past the queue for immigration and into the baggage hall, guiding me towards a row of seats by the big glass window overlooking the runway. And there, against the glare of the African sun, I spot my old friend.

JP's hair is greyer now, and the crow's feet around the eyes more pronounced. Despite all he's put himself through, he seems to be weathering pretty well. I grin, amused to note how he still sports the trademark black shirt and jeans that distinguish him as Le Trafiquant I remember. We shake hands, slapping each other awkwardly across the back. I'm hesitant. I suppose I'm not quite sure how recent events may have changed him.

'Sorry to keep you waiting,' I say. 'The plane was two hours late leaving.'

'Two hours in ten years makes little odds, my friend. Has Kebba taken your passport?'

'Oh, yes. I see you've thoroughly corrupted the system.'

JP squeezes my shoulder and winks. 'I give him work from time to time, so he owes me a favour or two. In Africa, it's good to know the men in suits. When you speak nicely to them, they give you useful things.'

He casually flicks the badge clipped to his shirt, and I tip my head for a closer look. Beneath the presidential crest is written: Head of Airport Security.

'Promotion, at last,' I say.

My passport is returned, opened at the page bearing the entry stamp and a scratched line in faded green ink, which I take to be the immigration officer's signature.

'I will get your baggage,' Kebba says. I describe it to him, and in mere seconds of small talk, we're all shuffling through customs with the same casual ease as I entered the country.

Back in the stultifying heat, Kebba brushes aside the fray of taxi hawks, money changers and beggars, until I almost collide with a wiry African blocking my way.

'This is Ousman,' JP shouts above the clamour. 'He's going to take us in his Land Rover.'

I shake Ousman's hand, immediately struck by the oddity of the woollen hat pulled firmly over his ears. He has Kebba load my bag onto the backseat of his Land Rover, and then Kebba and I do our best to squeeze in on either side of it. Ousman pushes the door against my shoulder in an effort to close it. I turn to peer into the back of the vehicle. Save for a balding spare wheel and a tin of oil, the voluminous luggage space bellows back with its sheer emptiness.

After about an hour's travelling south on a tarmac road, past empty fields and small villages, we pull off the road and take a dirt track alongside cultivated fields, bamboo and mango trees. We shudder to a stop in the rising dust, adjacent to a collection of huts. Ahead of us, a freshly whitewashed building occupies a site on the edge of an escarpment. Below are the beach and the ocean. I follow the line of the bay as it curves southwards, to where the waves break white and frothy on the rocky promontory.

'Well, this is it,' declares JP. 'This is my ice station.'

'An ice station?'

'Sure. It's like a gas station. Only, we sell ice.'

I flick the wobbly door catch and unfurl myself, taking an aching step or two as the blood circulates in my limbs. There's a pleasingly fresh sea breeze. Or maybe it's just that standing next to an ice station makes me feel cooler. Whichever it is, it's a welcome relief after being cooped up in the Land Rover.

His three employees emerge from the whitewashed building, and JP introduces me as his stranger from England. 'Welcome to Africa,' they chorus.

Musa, the plant manager, steps forward, offering his hand. 'What is your name?' he asks.

I tell him, and he repeats it, savouring the sound, as if tasting a previously undiscovered but appealing small fruit. 'This is your first time in Africa?'

'I've been before.'

They nod sagely.

'You'll like it here. Africa is not such a bad place.'

JP is squatting over a dismantled electric motor propped next to the entrance to the building. He sucks air between his teeth while probing the thick red wires coiled within the motor's casing. Judging by the body language, I fear the prognosis will not be good.

'Where is feeler gauge?' he holds up his palm. Musa places the measuring tool in his hand, and JP runs a thin blade around the inside of the casing until it jams. His shoulders stiffen. 'Musa!'

Musa slumps down beside him. 'Yes, Mr JP.'

'Why you let Wireman bring back electric motor when motor still no good?'

Now it's Musa's turn to suck air through his teeth. 'Why motor no good, Mr JP? Wireman tell me it's properly mended.'

'Look. Feeler gauge go get stuck between casing and will burn out motor again. This is no good for ice station. No good for Musa and Mr JP, and all the fishermen.'

'No good,' Musa repeats sotto voce. He takes the stuck gauge and wiggles it with a theatrical sigh. 'I call Wireman to take back motor. Tell him Mr JP plenty angry.'

'You do that. Plenty angry! And tell him Mr JP wants to talk with Wireman.' JP draws himself up to his full height, and Musa follows. The electric motor is left in the dirt, and a pair of scraggy chickens pick at it with their beaks.

'Come on.' JP grabs my bag, tossing it into a roofless, short-wheel-base Land Rover. 'Let's go get a drink.'

I clamber in after him, and when the engine finally coughs into life, he throws it in gear and we charge down the track, cutting through the escarpment to the beach.

'It can be very frustrating, this place,' he says, white knuckles gripping the steering wheel.

I want to tell him there are probably easier places in the world to make a living selling ice, but JP knows that stuff already, and I'm quite sure he doesn't need somebody fresh from England telling him something he already knows.

'There's the house up ahead. Proper Robinson Crusoe, don't you think?'

The Land Rover slews sideways in the deep sand, pebbles clattering the wheel arches. A line of baobab trees and stubby palms run parallel to the beach. Beyond them stands a white, single-storey house with bougainvillea and jacaranda plants clinging to its walls. At the corner of the house, the propeller of a small windmill is a blur of movement, and JP explains how it generates power to a twelve-volt battery in the awning of the roof.

He stops next to a small block building, freshly whitewashed. 'This is the toilet and shower,' he says. 'Come on. Follow me.'

He leads the short distance to where a two-metre-high tunnel has been bored into the escarpment. Inside, it is dark, humid and cool.

'I did this with a pick and shovel,' he says, running a hand over the curved earth sides.

I follow him deeper into the tunnel, and after about four metres, come to a well excavated to the level of the water table. I stare down into the well, but it's too dark to see any water. With my fingers, I dig a pebble from the mud wall and drop it in the hole. I count almost to three before there's a plopping sound. 'You did all this with a pick?'

'Sure.' He kicks a coil of rope attached to a tyre inner tube fashioned into a bucket. 'This is how we get water round here.'

'Isn't it salty?'

'Nah.' He points to the ocean. 'If you want salty, there's plenty out there.' We leave the tunnel, and he unlocks the green metal door to the house, ushering me into a spacious, simple room. The four barred windows have no glass, allowing a saline breeze to billow through the house.

Stacked along the wall are a series of wooden packing cases, a jumble of machinery parts, tools and operating manuals lying on top of them. Above the cases hang two oil paintings. One is of a prosperous-looking gentleman sternly contemplating all who cross the threshold. The other is of a group of Tuareg, the desert nomads of the Sahara. They are armed with swords and appear to be plotting their next ambush on some luckless traveller.

'You take the bedroom,' JP tells me.

'What about you?'

'I'll sleep here.' He scuffs his sandal on the rug in the middle of the room. 'I've been looking forward to it.'

I go and fetch my bag, dropping it in the bedroom. Unzipping it, I look around for somewhere to put my things. There are no drawers, cupboards or hooks, so I close the flap and zip it up again. Leaving the room, I pass a small table by the bed where a candle, a torch and a machete are laid. By the machete's long blade is an ornate seashell with crumpled cigarette butts in its smooth hollow. I pick up the machete, weighing it in my hands. From the sheen on the steel, it appears to have been recently sharpened. I wander from the bedroom.

'Is this really necessary?'

JP sits at his desk. He tilts his head forward and gazes over the top of his reading glasses. 'You never know.'

'Have you ever needed it?'

'Not so far.'

JP goes back to whatever he's doing at his desk, and I take a slow swing with the machete from left to right, almost decapitating a particularly large insect.

'I've never been a guest where weapons are supplied,' I tell him, turning back into the room. 'I appreciate your thoughtfulness.'

The salty breeze carries the whiff of fish from the smokehouse. It isn't unpleasant, but occasionally, it's accompanied by a more pungent stench. From the window, some distance along the beach, I can see the brightly painted pirogues rocking at their moorings. Fishermen unload large boxes, their legs forcing passage through the shallow, surging surf to the shore. Higher up the beach, others unpack the fish from the boxes, laying them on makeshift racks to dry in the sun.

'Those are my clients.' JP stands by the door behind me. 'They buy my ice.'

'And what's the place over there?' I point to a building rising above the thatched roofs.

'The bloody Japanese provided funding for a new ice station. They're the new competition.' He raises his hand and shakes a carton of Don Fernando red wine. 'This stuff's a bit rough, but it'll help wash away the dust.'

We sit with our backs against the wall of the house, looking south into the crescent of the bay and the promontory where the sea breaks white on the rocks. The propeller on the windmill at the corner of the house clicks as it spins, and the bougainvillea sway in the wind. The sun is low now. Soon, it will take its heat and its light and disappear beyond the ocean.

'What a place this is,' I say. 'What on earth brought you here?'

'Opportunity.'

I shoot him a sideways look.

'You shouldn't be so surprised. There's opportunity in a place like this.' He takes a long drink of his wine and places the glass back on the table. 'Hell, I'm finished with all that other stuff. Nobody deals straight these days. Fish and ice are safer. When we finally saw sense, me and a friend bought a trawler in Europe and steamed it all the way here. We fished the coast, landing our catch out there because we couldn't cross the reef.' He nods toward the waves breaking over the rocks in the middle of the bay. 'We hired canoes from the local people to bring the fish to the beach.

'In front of the house here, we built a drying platform. Then we built the house, the washhouse and the tunnel in the escarpment there. We made fine money with that trawler. Eventually, we sold it for a good price to some people from the south. Only, we didn't have any more fish to dry. That's when I came up with the ice idea. I said to my friend Jules we should build an ice station for the local fishermen. If they had ice, I told him, they would have better quality fish and get more money for it. But Jules, he wasn't so interested. He wanted to become a farmer, growing mangoes and bananas.' He flicks a hand dismissively at the patch of scrub beneath the trees. 'Except, the bloody monkeys kept eating them. Every time he planted more stuff, they'd eat it. I don't think he ever ate one of his own bananas. He was never quick enough.'

'I guess he had to give in to the monkeys,' I say.

'I told him he was wasting his time. We should do ice, I said. Monkeys don't eat ice. But he was too far gone by then. He went back to Europe to build a house for himself and his girlfriend. I don't think he'll be back.' JP grins, leaning towards me. 'You know, he used to sit out there with traps waiting for them, day and night. The monkeys watched him from the trees, tormenting him. One day, he came into the house all worked up with himself and said to me, "JP, I'm going to buy myself a gorilla suit in Europe. I'm going to dress up in it and sit out there under those big baobab trees, just like a goddamn scarecrow." He always reckoned monkeys were afraid of gorillas.'

I chuckle at the image I conjure in my mind. 'And did it work?'

'Did it hell. The crazy son of a bitch. And you know what? I've hardly seen a monkey since he left.' After the second carton of Don Fernando is finished, JP cooks some ladyfish in a pan by the dull glow of the strip light powered by the wind. He takes a sprinkling of chopped herbs from a plastic bag he keeps in a tin and tosses it over the sizzling fish. They throw off a sweet, pungent aroma.

'That smells great,' I say, bending over the pan.

JP flips over the fish. 'You bet. African herbs are the best.'

We tuck in, and the food tastes delicious after the long journey and all the talking and the wine.

'On my trawler, I used to have a dog...' JP pauses when a grey- and dark-striped cat slinks in from the night. He throws it some fish from his plate. 'The dog was a black mongrel we found outside a bar in Amsterdam. We called him La Roussette, which means 'dogfish' in French.' JP pushes his empty plate to the side. 'He liked nothing better than watching the fish come up in the net. And he was the best port watch I ever had. Nobody got on that boat without La Roussette's permission. I even had a goat at one time. Yeah, we were a proper Noah's Ark back then. Jules bought the goat in a market in Djibouti, so we'd have fresh meat for the voyage. Only, he became part of the crew. After a while, none of us had the heart to eat him. He and La Roussette were big pals.

'Unfortunately, the goat broke his leg in a heavy sea. He'd been out on the deck eating his straw. I taped a metal pipe to his leg, but it wouldn't hold. He was finished. I took him to the bow and bled him into the sea and threw his carcass over as a sacrifice to the gods. It broke La Roussette's heart. But we got some good fishing after that.'

. . .

DAWN BREAKS COOL AND CLEAR. I wash with a bucket of cool water I've hauled from the well in the tunnel. It's very refreshing, and I tip the last half of it over my head to wash away the soap. JP has already gone to his ice station, and I've agreed to meet him there later. Then he's promised a visit to meet Stanley, who he describes as a mad bush scientist who helps him out from time to time.

The same grey- and dark-striped cat that visited us the previous evening is back for his breakfast. After I dress, I take a coffee and a chunk of the leftover ladyfish from the pan and go outside. Those herbs still smell damn good. The cat devours the fish before it's barely left my hand. JP says she has three kittens hidden at the ice plant and is always begging for food. Still licking her lips, she creeps along the base of the jacaranda. In a blur of movement, she sinks her teeth into the head of a sizeable gecko, whose tail flicks in the dirt while its legs paddle futilely in the air. There's a faint crack, and it's all over for the gecko.

'Where is JP?'

The booming voice has me leaping from my skin. Spinning round, I scowl at the oval face of a tall and imposing African. 'The ice station,' I snap.

The man turns his head casually, looking somewhat incongruous in his dark suit and dark glasses. 'How do I get there?'

I indicate with my outstretched hand to where the line of baobab trees and brushwood meet the track leading up the escarpment. 'It's above the track. On the edge of the escarpment.'

He fingers his tie, gazing at the dust already soiling his shoes. 'When is he back?'

'Not 'til later. I'm supposed to meet him there in one hour, and then we're going to see Stanley.'

'Stanley?'

'He's a...' I refrain from adding the mad bush scientist bit because I've never met this guy before. Neither have I met Stanley, for that matter. Who is most probably not mad at all. 'I've only just arrived,' I tell him.

'I know. From England.'

I frown, somewhat taken aback. 'How news travels,' I say.

'It does, my friend. I am the Commander of the National Intelligence Agency.'

The National Intelligence Agency? My heart skips a beat for the second time in as many minutes. This guy's full of surprises. But wait a minute... why is the chief of the spy station personally visiting JP's beach?

'My name is Mohammed,' he announces, thrusting out a big hand. I take the firm, cool grip, gawping at my convex head in the lenses of his sunglasses. I can see the maker's name etched on the right lens.

Just as I begin to wonder if Mohammed will ever release my hand, he does so, immediately dropping into one of the plastic chairs. He taps the adjacent chair for me to sit next to him and, for what seems an eternity, remains utterly inert. His face has become a mask, his attention drawn to the rough ground where Jules once made his stand against the monkeys. He puts me in mind of those police computers that, in seconds, scan hundreds of mug shots, attempting to match the culprit and his nefarious pursuits. Is Mohammed looking for my photo somewhere up there in that forehead of his?

The plastic chair flexes when the commander leans to his side and faces me.

'JP has something for me,' he says. A wave of garlic breath explodes against my face. 'You see, the barrel has snapped. In Africa, a replacement barrel is never easy to come by.'

A snapped barrel. My mind whirls. Is this a coded message? Is this how arms dealers open all their transactions?

His eyes interrogate mine.

'I wasn't sure if he'd asked you to bring it, you see. From England.'

'Absolutely not!'

A hand darts inside his jacket. I tense, convinced he's reaching for a gun. I clench my jaw, fearing more gun-toting agents about to spring from behind these baobabs.

When his hand reappears, it's cradling the broken pieces of a pipe. 'I know JP has a spare one I can borrow. Do you like to smoke a pipe?'

I draw a deep breath and exhale. 'Not much help there, I'm afraid.'

'Pity. I love to smoke my pipe. I'll just have to wait.' After returning the broken pieces to the inside pocket of his jacket, he knits his fingers, stretching his legs in the sand. 'You know, people say certain specimens were possibly around before the birth of Christ. That would make them the oldest living relics of ancient times.'

He's lost me again.

He nods in the direction of the baobab trees. 'One of the largest baobabs in Africa has a circumference of nearly forty-seven metres. People live in them. Store grain in them. Oh, they are one of nature's great wonders.' His hand clamps my forearm. 'I once read of a Major Trollip. In the Second World War, this Major Trollip built a fully operative toilet in the hollow of such a magnificent tree. And it still exists today. It is known as the "Toilet Tree".' The commander rumbles into a booming laugh. When he's quite recovered, he says, 'He must have been British, this Major Trollip, don't you think?'

'Most probably,' I say.

'Only the British are capable of such humour.' His grip tightens on my forearm. 'How long are you here for?'

'A few days.'

'And why are you here?'

'JP is an old friend. And I haven't seen him for many years.'

He nods his head. 'You will like it here.' He releases my forearm, springing to his feet. 'Now I must go. Tell JP to call me.'

Later, when I get to the track leading up the escarpment, I notice a fisherman standing at the edge of the surf. He's holding a long fishing rod in both hands, and he doesn't seem to want to let me out of his sight. For a moment or two, we watch each other. I wave. He doesn't. I decide there's something odd about him, but right now, I can't put my finger on what it is. A dark green car is parked close to the foot of the escarpment with another rod leaning against the side of it, and I assume it's his car. As I walk up the track, I stop suddenly to look back. He's still watching me.

Outside JP's factory, the electric motor with the big red wires lies propped against the wall. Wireman has not returned. The ground around it has been pecked clean by the chickens. 'Did you sleep well?' JP is rubbing his hands on a strip of filthy rag.

'Great. A guy called Mohammed came looking for a pipe.'

'Mohammed?'

'The head of intelligence.'

He pulls a face. 'He wanted a pipe? A smoking pipe?'

'You have to call him.'

JP shakes his head. 'I never knew he smoked.'

'He does now.' 'Did you see the guy on the beach?'

Ping! Now I realise what looked so out of place: 'Do all the fishermen round here wear those enormous binoculars when fishing from the beach?'

'I never saw anyone fish from that beach before. Maybe he's a diamond smuggler hiding out.' 'Why on earth would he be a diamond smuggler? It's quite conceivable he's someone on holiday who likes catching fish from the beach.' JP throws the filthy rag on the electric motor. 'Hey, Musa! That man, he still on beach, fishing?' Musa frowns. 'He came last night. After dusk.' 'Why don't you go ask him what the hell he's doing down there?' 'He's fishing, JP.'

'You think so?'

'I don't think he's from government, if that's what you mean.' JP waves a dismissive hand, and we go inside the building. High up are two big silver boxes with a confusion of pipes. These are the ice makers, he explains. Beneath them is a shredder through which the ice falls, and the flake ice is then channelled into a refrigerated container below, where it stays until the fishermen bring their boats to the beach. A couple of medium-sized diesel engines power a generator, and a switchboard controls the ice makers and the cooling plant for the container. Several engines are dotted about, and JP describes each in substantial detail, including their provenance, running hours, circumstances and future prospects, as if they may have been an extension of his family. He runs a hand over each of them, and I imagine he is at his most content in the company of his engines. A curious notion occurs to me as I listen to him, and it is that he is here in the African bush, not particularly to make ice and sell it to the fishermen, but that this whole enterprise has more to do with finding a purpose for his engines, keeping them occupied, maintained and running. From that alone, he will seek his reward. That alone will satisfy his intent.

We finish the tour standing at the edge of the escarpment, looking down at the beach and the sea.

'This is what I really want.' JP throws out his arms. 'I want this bay.'

From up here, I have a better view of where the waves wash over the reef.

'And what do you want to do with it?' He describes the rondavels he'll build for the tourists and where he'll place them among the baobab trees, so they'll be protected from the wind and close to the ocean. He describes the wood and thatch and palm frond he'll use to make them. Then he points to his house, which will be a restaurant and bar, and there'll be an open fire to grill the meat and the fish.

'My clients will go out in the pirogues with the fishermen,' he says. 'They can catch their own food, relax in the bar, and watch the sun sink into the ocean. It'd be a hell of a place.'

'Plenty of ice for the cocktails.'

'Plenty of ice for everyone.'

We climb into the roofless Land Rover and return along the dirt track we came on yesterday. Crossing the road, we follow a maze of bumpy trails that draw us into the heart of rural African life in all its virtuous simplicity. I smell the burning wood of the cooking fires and see the neat mud-brick houses, the small crop cultivations, the calling children and the women in their gaily-coloured traditional dress going about their chores. We pass similar scenes, until JP stops outside a metal gate in the centre of a white wall. He honks the horn. The gate partially opens, and a face appears.

'Hello, Mr JP,' the man says, drawing back the gate.

We pull into the compound, parking next to a hole in the ground. 'This is going to be the swimming pool,' JP explains.

I take in the single-storey residence in the centre of the compound, the staff accommodation block adjacent to the perimeter wall, the expanse of garden in a state of establishment, the tall palms and the variegated creepers, and the vegetable garden in the far corner.

Stanley, the mad bush scientist, emerges from the shade of his garage wearing white oil-stained fatigues and a T-shirt. He has a shock of unkempt hair and a middle-aged, cheerful face with a black streak on one cheek, just below the eye. He wipes the streak with the back of his hand, smearing grease over his cheekbone. I'm unsure if they're a pair of sandals flapping on his feet, or an old pair of shoes in the final moments of disintegration. There is little evidence of Stanley's madness on first pass. Besides, I imagine a state of madness is a relative and rather intangible condition, out here in the bush.

After introductions, Stanley leads us into his workshop. From melted pistons, all donated by JP, he and his two assistants are casting a replacement casing for the side of a motorcycle engine. In his Geordie accent, Stanley explains how the first batch of pistons he'd tried to melt exploded, due to their metallic compound. He sheepishly draws our attention to an expanse of scorched and pitted wall. The mould was rendered useless in the explosion, so it's back to square one.

'When something doesn't work,' Stanley laments, 'I just say sod it, and I go fetch myself another bottle of beer. Would you lads like one?'

We agree to join him. It's obviously been one of those mornings for Stanley. I count two empty beer bottles on his workbench already, and it's not yet midday.

Stanley reappears with three bottles of beer. 'Come on, lads. I'll show you the property.'

I savour a mouthful of the refreshing beer and follow Stanley out of his workshop, the two assistants tagging along behind so that a small, human procession meanders through the vegetable garden. We stand around two large solar panels, the colour of charcoal.

'To optimise the energy input from the sun, I've put a small sensor on each of the panels, which detects the energy levels and follows the sun through its arc. These sensors send a signal down to a motor under the panels, which drives a set of gear wheels taken from a bicycle.' Stanley sinks to his knees. 'These motors are out of video players, and together with the gear wheels, they drive the panels like this.' Stanley blocks the sunlight to one of the sensors with his hand, which causes the solar panel to jerk into life. It clicks and whirrs, flicking back and forth like an electronic junkie craving a fix.

'Not bad, eh? Bit of lateral thinking, that's all it takes out here.'

Stanley climbs back to his feet, and the solar panel stops clicking and whirring, returning to a state of Zen-like calm. We move on to the next invention, a water pump made from parts never designed to be in a water pump.

As the grand tour draws to a close, the finale is the irrigation system, fabricated from a collection of intravenous drips. We retire to the shade of Stanley's veranda at the back of the house and drink the rest of our beer. The alcohol puts me in a reflective mood, and I marvel at the resourcefulness of Stanley, who can come to such a place as this and create what he has.

JP puts his empty bottle on the table with a crack. 'Why don't we get something to eat at Yoro's bar?' he suggests. 'I'm getting hungry.'

'Count me in.' Stanley drains his beer and shouts through an open window. 'I'm just getting some lunch, love!'

Yoro's bar is a short stroll from JP's house, adjacent to the fish drying racks, and close to where the colourful pirogues are pulled up on the beach. The bar is built around a baobab tree, and I imagine Mohammed, the Commander of the Intelligence Agency, would be suitably impressed by how the tree has been used. The floor is made from baked earth, the roof from palm leaves, and the wind blows unchecked through its core. Two hammocks made from fishing nets hang limply between the tree and the bar. Some of the fishermen from the north, from Senegal, apparently frequent it for the food, the drink and the company. Though the bar is run by Yoro, it belongs to a German with a sport-fishing boat moored in the bay. He comes occasionally from Europe to drink his beer and catch the barracuda that are plentiful out beyond the reef during the season. JP points out the two chameleons watching from the rafters below the palm leaves, dragging their bellies and slowly turning their prehistoric heads.

'The fishermen joke with Yoro that these two creatures are spirits influenced by the old German,' JP says. 'They've been sent to watch over his bar.'

By all accounts, Yoro once tried to cast them into the

bush. The fishermen told him bad things would come to him and his family if he did such a thing, and so the chameleons continue to watch over the bar for the old German.

Stanley, JP and I order a plate of smoked fish with rice and a spicy sauce. We dig in with our spoons and talk to the fishermen about their catch and why all the fish disappear when the wind blows. By mid-afternoon, JP has to get back to his ice station to await Wireman's arrival, and Stanley thinks he should probably return to his wife. We make our farewells to the fishermen and leave.

I'VE no idea how long I slept. Laid against an upturned boat reading, I was lulled to sleep by the sound of the rolling surf. The sun has already begun its fall over the ocean.

JP has returned. He's sitting in one of the plastic chairs with his back against the wall of the house, tamping bits of tobacco into his pipe, lighting it and looking pensive.

'You should have woken me,' I tell him.

'You seemed very comfortable.'

I get to my feet and look down the beach as I stretch. Beyond the undergrowth, I make out the man with his fishing rod standing by his car. He's facing in our direction.

'He still there?' JP asks.

'Yeah. And your electric motor?' 'That son of a bitch is still there, too.'

'Wireman never came, huh?'

'He never did.'

'Bad wireman,' I mumble, returning to my view of the beach. 'I wonder what that guy is catching?'

'I haven't a goddamn clue. But he needn't have to wear binoculars to do it.' JP rasps a finger against his cheek, and smoke whirls up his face. 'He shouldn't be on my damn beach.'

'Can you see fish with binoculars?'

'I never tried.'

I wash the grogginess from my head, scooping the sun-warmed water from the bucket onto my face and dry myself with the bottom of my shirt. My ablutions have already assumed a rather elementary form.

Settling in the chair beside JP, I inhale the sweet aroma of tobacco. He seems to be visibly relaxing with each puff.

'I'm gonna beat that guy's brains out tomorrow,' he says, squeezing the bowl of his pipe.

I presume he means the electrician, rather than the fisherman. 'With the electric motor?'

'Sure. Why not? By the way, we ran out of booze. Why don't we go back to Yoro's bar and get more? We can see if Yellowman is there. Tell him to take us fishing out beyond the reef. It's the wrong season for barracuda, but you never know what else we might find out there.'

'Yeah, let's do that.'

JP locks the house, and we stroll down the beach in the gathering darkness.

'Is he really yellow, this guy with the boat?' I'm beginning to believe anything is possible in this place.

'You'll see.'

Some fishermen from the north sit at one of the tables in the bar, their profiles silhouetted against the closing light to the west, and the whites of their eyes reflect in the muted glow of the naked lightbulb. Bottles of Guinness rest on the tabletop, and they talk energetically. 'Hello, JP,' they chorus, taking turns to shake his hand. 'Welcome to Africa,' they say to me, followed by, 'Is this your first time?' And then they pour their attention back on JP: 'When you going to have ice for us, Mr JP? The Japanese can't make enough ice in this hot weather. When they haven't enough ice, they always favour the local fishermen before us.'

JP throws up his hands. 'Hey, guys! Why does the white man have to mend African politics?'

They tell him that if the white man hadn't come to Africa in the first place, with all his manner of inventions and machinery, so-called progressive ideas and great expectations, then perhaps African politics wouldn't need mending.

'Bullshit!' JP responds. 'Listen, my friends. When Wireman comes to mend my motor, then we will all have ice. And peace will return to our little corner of Africa.'

We retire to a quiet table at the other side of the bar, while the Africans continue their drinking, their smoking and their energetic conversation. On the makeshift bar, an old stereo plays soft music, and Yoro brings over a carton of Don Fernando and two pewter cups.

'Hello, JP. Do you not know me in this darkness?'

'Hello, Lamin,' he says after a moment. 'It is true; I did not recognise you. How are you? This is my stranger from England.'

We shake hands. Lamin is a policeman. 'Where have you been, JP? I haven't seen you for a long time.' 'I had to go travelling, but I've been back a while. I came looking for you. You don't come in the bar so much these days.' 'I've been in the south. The rebels are active again, so many refugees are coming north. We are trying to accommodate them in camps down the road, but it is not easy. The facilities are very poor. We can barely feed them, let alone help the injured. There is a big offensive coming. You will hear the guns soon, maybe as early as tomorrow. I think the president must be worried. I fear the fighting will eventually end up here.' Lamin smiles. 'And I'm not so sure the rebels will buy your ice.'

The evening wind crackles the thatched palms above our heads, and the shadows dodge and weave in tune with the lightbulb swinging lazily on its cord. For a moment, we are silent in the low light, watching the fishermen leave the bar, their forms melting into the darkness, their voices the only indication of their lingering presence.

'Lamin?'

'Yes, JP.'

'Who do the police say killed Tomsen, the Scandinavian man?'

'I wasn't involved in the case because I have been at the border, as I said. I heard there was confusion. In the end, it seems he killed himself. It seems he put the pistol to his own head and pulled the trigger.'

'So, they don't think he was murdered?'

'No, JP. The case is finished; he won't be troubling anyone. Did you recover all the things he took?'

'It doesn't matter about the things.'

'All the same, he shouldn't have done that.'

'Don't they think it was strange that the pistol was on the other side of the room from the body, and that the door was locked from the outside?'

'These things happen, JP. Perhaps it was influenced by the spirits. They can be like that when they want. You know, he came to the village drunk one night and said very bad things about the shaman. Perhaps it would have been better if he had not said those things. Anyway, the case is closed. You should not concern yourself. Does it concern you?'

'No.'

'Have you a problem with your ice station?

'A motor burnt out, so the plant is not working.'

'I heard that. That's not so good. Now the Japanese take all the business.'

'Yeah, I know.' JP upends his cup. 'Maybe I should tell the shaman.'

Somewhere in the dark, a motorcycle roars into life. There is a flash of light on metal as it charges through the dull glow of the bulb. The fishermen stumble back into the bar, arm in arm, laughing. Lamin asks them where the man on the motorcycle is going, as if, in his position as lawman, he might consider detaining him. 'He is drunk,' they say. 'Gone home to sleep it off.'

'But he's gone in the wrong direction,' JP points out. 'He isn't going to sleep too well in the ocean.'

One of the fishermen splutters, flailing his arms as if pretending to swim, and once again, they are helpless with laughter.

Ignoring the fishermen, JP leans forward, resting his elbows on the bench. 'There is a man on the beach, Lamin. He stands by his car pretending to fish when all he is doing is watching. Who is he?' Lamin clears his throat. 'I don't know who you mean. Perhaps he is from the government.'

'Does the president think JP will attempt a *coup d'etat*? What does he think I'm gonna do, pack him in ice and freeze him to death?'

'I don't suppose so. Anyway, I must leave you now.'

'Hey, Lamin. Come for lunch tomorrow, my friend. Some of the people are coming.'

'Thank you. I will try. Have a good evening, JP.' He nods in my direction, and with that, Lamin disappears into the night.

JP turns to the bar. 'Hey, Yoro,' he calls. 'Where is Yellowman?'

. . .

BOOM!

I groggily snatch my watch from the bedside table, half opening an eye. It's eight o'clock in the morning. Through the window, the sun is well above the escarpment, and the sky is clear blue. Yet thunder rumbles.

Thunder?

I roll onto my back. Placing my palms on each temple, I gently massage the hangover. Man, that wine is rough. Don Fernando himself is marching around my head, banging the most enormous set of drums.

BOOM! CRACK!

I spring upright on the bed. That's not thunder. And neither is it coming from inside my head.

BOOM!

I scrabble out of bed, pulling on my desert boots. Instinct tells me to grab the machete on the way out. In the main room, I tiptoe past the inert form of JP. It's inconceivable how he sleeps through this din. Stealthily, I open the door.

BOOM!

My heart thumps faster as I venture outside. Lamin was right. This is the sound of heavy artillery coming from across the southern border. The rebel offensive must have started. I walk down to where the surf foams against the sand, passing the dead fish washed up on the last tide. Flapping, bald-necked vultures peck at the eyeless bodies. Along the beach, some of the pirogues are already heading out to sea. Fishermen are wading through the surf, lugging equipment for the other boats still at their moorings. Men are bent over in the pirogues, arranging their gear for the coming day. There's a group of five people sitting on the beach mending nets. Palls of smoke rise from the cooking fires. People are meandering, not running, not frantically loading their possessions into those old, growling trucks belching their filthy black smoke and heading north. How come nobody seems worried? It says so much about the African spirit – they get on with life as best they can.

BOOM!

'Good morning, Mista!'

I spin round. Where on earth has this guy surfaced from? Rastafarian dreadlocks dangle from a woolly hat. Bulging, woven bags hang from each shoulder. The sun glints off the half-dozen silver and gold watches strapped between his wrist and his elbow.

'How are you today, my friend?'

I tell him I'm very well, though I doubt he believes me, dressed as I am in crumpled T-shirt, underpants and gaping boots. While gazing at the machete hanging from my hand, he hooks a pair of wraparound sunglasses from the breast pocket of his Hawaiian shirt.

'I think you need a pair of Terminator shades, man,' he offers cheerfully. Another set of sunglasses are conjured from a woven bag. 'Or maybe you prefer the Miami Vice look. Like Sonny Crockett. Yeah, he's the man.'

As if to augment his sales patter, a tune of sorts drifts from between his toothy grin. I'm no expert, yet I suspect he's mixing the soundtrack from *Miami Vice* with the one from *Beverly Hills Cop*. However, right at this moment, I really don't care.

I shake my head, attempting to comprehend what's taking place here. 'This is so bizarre,' I mutter under my breath.

'Yes, my friend. I got it all. My name is Bargain Bob. And I'm truly a walking BAZAAR!'

I gape at Bargain Bob, rummaging in one of the bags. A

fake leopard skin purse and a handful of bracelets fall on the sand. I certainly have no need for those.

'You want a bargain watch, man? Look, I show you.' He thrusts out his forearm. 'All of them made in Switzerland. Top quality.'

'Not today, Bob.'

'Maybe something for the lady?'

I stomp back through the sand, curling my toes to not shed my unlaced boots as I go. I've read of this conflict as being a low-level civil war waged between the government of Senegal and the Movement of Democratic Forces of Casamance. Since 1990, the mostly Jola people have been fighting for independence of the Casamance region.

Though, low-level is not how I'd describe this racket.

As I pass the corner of the house, the propeller on the windmill is clicking in the warm breeze blowing off the sea. JP will know what to do. I need to wake him up. As I approach the door, I hear the bleating of an animal drift from within.

I stop dead when JP emerges from the doorway smiling blissfully and hitching the belt on his trousers. 'Ah, what a beautiful day,' he says.

Barely has he emerged into the sunshine than a brown and white goat prances from the doorway, followed by a youth with a two-handed grip on the rope attached to its neck.

'You look like you've seen a ghost.'

'I've seen a goat,' I mutter.

'What?'

'Well, it's not every day you wake up in a warzone. I mean...'

'Ach! They'll blow themselves out by lunchtime. You won't need that machete today.' He nods toward the goat, now nibbling leaves beneath the jacaranda tree. 'Plenty of meat on her, don't you think?'

'You mean you're going to eat her?'

'Sure. I bought her from this farmer for my lunch guests.'

After I've washed and dressed, I take a strong coffee on the terrace with JP. If Wireman won't come for the electric motor, JP is saying, then he will take it to the son of a bitch himself. He'd be gone a couple of hours. I tell him I will take a walk down the road to the bird sanctuary, about three kilometres away, returning along the beach by the mangrove swamps.

He slams the Land Rover door shut, revving the engine. 'Don't forget, lunch is at one.'

How could I forget? I cast the goat a forlorn look.

I'm about to leave when a man wanders around the corner of the house. I do a double-take when I clap eyes on him. He's decked out in yellow sou'wester and yellow waterproof trousers. The black Wellington boots make giant footprints in the sand.

'Hello,' he says softly. 'I'm Yellowman.'

I'm glad this little mystery's been solved, at least. I look him over. Scales and old fish blood coat the front of his smock.

'I hear you're the best fisherman in the bay,' I tell him, after introducing myself.

He neither denies nor admits my attempt at flattery. I reckon he's cautiously hedging his bets. Fishing being what it is, I imagine it could be bad juju to exhibit an overconfidence in one's ability. Instead, he asks, 'This your first time in Africa?'

I tell him I've been here before.

'Where is JP?'

'Gone to see Wireman with his motor.'

He nods his head knowingly. By now, I imagine everyone must know about the broken electrical motor.

'When d'you want to go fishing?'

'How about the morning?'

He nods again. 'I will come back tomorrow.'

I look him up and down in all his heavy-weather gear, presuming he's just returned from a morning's fishing. 'I hope you left something out there for us.'

He looks at me blankly. 'There's no fishing today, boss.'

After Yellowman has left, I follow the path beneath the baobabs, towards the track up the escarpment, making a shortcut by scrambling up a narrow gully and using the exposed tree roots to propel myself up. Through the foliage, I see the man standing by his car on the beach. I watch him for a while from the cover of the trees, enjoying the fact that he most likely can't see me. At last, I've got one over on him.

The walk takes all morning, and when I return, the guns have ceased their booming. I arrive from the back of the house, passing the empty goat skin. It puts me in mind of a bag that's been robbed and then flung aside by the thief. I think it's the machete from my bedside table laid in the patch of darkened dirt. The blood on the blade has dried a rusty brown.

Children are playing among the baobabs, chasing each other through the undergrowth, calling and waving sticks. They stop suddenly when they catch sight of me.

'Hello,' I say, and they run off behind the house, in the direction of adult voices.

I follow the smell of cooking and see cuts of the goat sizzling on a makeshift grill. I have to admit it smells very good. I don't know how many people JP invited. There must be thirty or forty milling about in the shade thrown by the trees. The women, a riot of colour in their national dress, squat on mats while preparing vegetables and semolina. The men stand around in slacks and open-neck shirts, chatting. Now they are closer to the adults, the children seem to have recovered sufficient courage to resume their game of tag. A couple of guys lean over the grill. They take a joint off the fire, set it aside on a big plate and begin slicing chunks of grey flesh from it, placing them in a terracotta bowl.

'Hey! How was the walk?' JP asks.

I think for a moment how to sum it up. In my brain, I have a flash review of all the faces, young and old, and their many questions and demands. It was exhausting. Much more tiring than the walking. For all of sixty seconds, I'd hidden in the mangrove swamp. They'd found me there, too.

'I was a thing of much curiosity,' I say.

JP grunts. 'Come. I'll introduce you to some of the guys.'

Lamin, the policeman, is here with his wife and two children. So is Kebba, the immigration man who so efficiently cleared me into the country. Others include a couple of soldiers of indeterminate rank, a youngish fellow from the security service sporting a fine beard, a very tall fireman, a man from a radio station, another policeman, several from the presidential guard, a couple of guys from one of the ministries (I forget which) and a short fellow with enormously thick lenses, from the meteorological department. They're a curious mix, and I'm suddenly struck with the not-so-happy thought that perhaps, for JP to secure the rights to this bay and get rid of the Japanese and their ice station into the bargain, he really is considering a *coup d'etat*. That's why the guy with his fishing rod and binoculars has been watching our comings and goings. These lunch guests will be JP's accomplices. He's got the army here, police force, communications, propaganda, a man to put out the fires. Only one thing baffles me: I'm not entirely clear where the fellow from the meteorological office fits in. How might a weather forecast be incumbent upon a successful coup?

Perhaps I should tread warily. Though, they certainly don't appear like plotters, as they tuck into lunch in the company of their families. But I suppose that's what plotters do the world over. One minute they're eating couscous with their families, and the next – BLAM – they're off, firing their guns and causing untold mayhem.

I decide to mingle, to see if I can detect an undercurrent of dissent. I work through some potential opening lines, such as: 'Quite noisy this morning, wasn't it?' Or maybe something a little lighter: 'We should eat up quickly before the rebels pinch it.'

On second thoughts, I think I'll just get something to eat.

The last guests leave just before sunset, and JP and I retire to our habitual place, sitting in the plastic chairs with our backs against the sun-warmed house. Don Fernando has joined us again. There's already a crumpled carton laid on the floor. JP has just come back from the house with his plastic bag of African herbs from the kitchen.

'We've got some fish to eat if you're hungry.'

'I'm all good,' I tell him, holding up my hands. 'The couscous was excellent.'

I watch him open the bag of herbs and sprinkle some among the neat line of tobacco he's already made on a strip of Rizla paper. In Indonesia, they put chives in their cigarettes, I remind myself, so maybe this isn't so strange.

'Aren't those the same herbs you put on the fish we ate the other night?'

'Sure.'

How curious. Does anybody back home think to add

herbs de Provence to their cigarettes? After all, they smell good enough to smoke. 'D'you often smoke these herbs, then?'

'I do when it's best African skunk.'

'No wonder that cat's always here. She's not only hungry. She's a bloody junkie.'

Rolling the cigarette carefully, he runs his tongue along the edge and seals it. He flicks the lighter, and there's a faint crackle as the tobacco and best African skunk ignite. He pulls a deep drag, and the sweet, pungent smoke fills the air.

'You want some?' He holds the joint towards me.

I hesitate. Normally, drugs don't interest me, especially when it comes with the unappealing name of 'skunk'. Don Fernando has weakened my resolve, though. He's already smothering me in his very agreeable alcoholic cloak.

I take a deep pull, doing my best to stifle the cough. I hold it for a second or two in my lungs and blow it out. I look around me. I feel nothing different.

'What's this supposed to do that Don Fernando can't?'

'Keep it. I'll make another one for myself.'

I take another drag... count to five... exhale... look around. Nothing. I reach for the glass of wine and slurp back a throat-quenching mouthful.

'So. I guess you're wondering what I was doing in that prison?' JP moistens the edge of the Rizla paper and lights it up.

'It had crossed my mind.'

He tips back his head and blows a stream of smoke into the night sky.

'I once met this mean Belgian mercenary in a bar in Antwerp. He told me there were a lot of opportunities on the Horn of Africa. He got me work on a boat from time to time. Nobody to call a friend, but he had some good stories to tell. I took his advice, gathered all my money and bought a trawler. Me, Jules and a mad cook called Max sailed that little boat through the Mediterranean and down through the Suez Canal, all the way until we reached Djibouti. It took a long time to make some contacts when we got there, and I suspected the old mercenary was full of crap. To earn money, Jules took on some building work, while I mended engines for the local fishermen. Max, he just got pissed. Then some guy gave us a contract to shift sheep to Saudi. We didn't much like it because they messed up the boat. But we needed the money. And we made Max clear up all the shit. At least cleaning all that crap stopped him drinking so much, and when he didn't drink so much, he managed to cook us something to eat. Eventually, we spread further afield with our cargoes, to Yemen and Somalia. Then, one day, we met this Arab guy with a bad smile and broken teeth, and things really started to take off...'

I want to stretch my legs, but I have lost all mobility. I'm urging them as best I can, yet nothing happens. They could just as well be stumps of dead wood protruding from my waist. I take a last drag before I'm in danger of singeing my fingers. I'm incapable of reaching the ashtray to stub this thing out. With intense concentration, I manage to transmit a feeble signal to my index finger and thumb for them to part. Just in time, the joint plummets, red and smoking. It's a Second World War fighter plane riddled by flack. The plane falls, turning and spinning, before crashing into the ocean with a splash. I blink twice and see the joint hissing as it whirls in a saucer of milk left out for the cat.

'...then things changed a little when we took a cargo of hash from Pakistan and offloaded it to a freighter in the Seychelles. We made some good money after that. I said to

Jules, "You know, Jules, we could make more money at this if we took the cargo ourselves to Europe." And so, we did.

'I worked like hell to keep that trawler's engine chugging away. It was wonderful. We sailed that little boat all the way round Africa, far out into the southern Atlantic, into the fabled Roaring Forties, and then up north, up the central Atlantic. We used to do all our refuelling from tankers out at sea, and we never touched land the whole way.

'We often hit a lot of bad weather, blown all over the place we were. And that little engine gave me a few sleepless nights, I can tell you. But what an adventure. That engine was a Werkspoor...'

JP is swaying in his chair, though I suspect, in reality, he's sitting perfectly still. I need some more wine for my parched throat. I try moving my arm from where it rests on the chair, though it resists all commands. I'm concentrating hard, gawping at my hand when, all of a sudden, it's off, propelled on a trajectory that will send the wine glass, ashtray and carton of wine clattering against the wall. Miraculously, it stops in time, though I haven't the faintest idea how I will get that glass successfully back to my lips. On the wine carton, Don Fernando has removed the cape from his shoulders. He's wiggling it in front of himself like a bullfighter. Is he trying to provoke me?

'...are you okay?'

I gawp at JP, my eyeballs bouncing upward as if they're the line of symbols in a penny slot machine. 'I'm... absolutely... fine,' I lie.

Talking is akin to chewing toffee, my voice sounding as if it's reverberating along a very long tunnel. I could be shouting from the bottom of JP's well.

'Little did we know that the authorities had finally got on to us. Despite all our cunning efforts, they were tracking us with some of the most expensive surveillance equipment in the world: satellites and AWACs and the like. In the end, there was no way we could evade them. We'd really pissed somebody off. They finally got us on a beach in the Baltic, just as we were unloading the stash. The army, the navy, the intelligence service, they all descended on us that day, with all their boats and their helicopters. It was chaos. We were something of a cause célèbre at the time – the famous hash smugglers. Then we had the court case...'

In a flash, JP's chin has grown long and thin, the top of his head pointed. The colour of his whole head is crimson red. Wow! Now he's normal again, talking about the court case, wobbling in his chair like a human jelly. I want to talk. I want to know the value of the hash he was smuggling and what happened to his boat. It's suddenly terribly important to know what happened to his boat. Yet, my lips are sealed. I'm trapped in this husk of a body.

'...and after the case, I got three years, with the first year in solitary confinement. One of the guys told me later they couldn't believe where we'd been in that little trawler. We were only caught in the end because our client betrayed us. Anyway, I'm finished with all that stuff. Ice is what I do now...'

URGH! I blink twice before lifting my trousers off my face and tossing them onto the floor. I'm in the bedroom, and it's light outside. I gaze around me. The room is square. The bars in the window are straight. I'm holding four fingers and one thumb in front of my face. Therefore, I must be alive.

I roll onto my back, scratching my skull with the fingernails of both hands, trawling my memory. Gradually, the fog clears. I remember getting out of the chair last night with an enormous sense of purpose and hauling myself up a steep incline to the house, grabbing at the jacaranda and bougainvillea to propel me upward. If I'm not mistaken – yes, that's right – the house had no longer been on the ground, but high up in a tree. Once I'd climbed inside, my feet had scraped across the room, and for some time, I was a deep-sea diver, lugging my lead boots across the seafloor. The journey had seemed interminable. On the way, I talked with a group of Tuaregs camping in the desert, and then I'd met a very smart gentleman, who'd refused to utter one single word in response. Unimpressed, I'd laid down on the bed, half undressed, shaking violently until falling asleep.

I wait a moment to see if anything else from last night comes back to me. It doesn't. Okay, I tell myself, let's just hope that was all a bad dream.

I swing my legs off the bed, and a boot falls off my left foot. For some reason, the bedside table is pressed against the door. I move it and open the door. JP is not on the rug in the middle of the room. The door to the outside is open. I smell fresh coffee. My first few steps are a little unsteady, and then I'm away, passing the painting of the Tuaregs, with whom I enjoyed such a pleasant discussion, followed by the man who wouldn't say a thing.

'There's fresh coffee in the pot,' JP shouts from outside.

I take a mug out of the sink and half fill it, dropping in two sugars and stirring it with a knife. Not even the short stroll across the room has shaken the mood of apprehension, the sense of imminent doom. I'm sure Mohammed, the Commander of the National Intelligence Agency, will descend upon us any moment with his gang of heavies. They'll uncover JP's stash of African herbs, and it'll be curtains: no way back, ten years breaking rocks.

Outside, JP is sitting in one of the plastic chairs smoking his pipe, a mug of coffee steaming on the table next to him.

I drop into the other chair. 'You been up long?'

'Nah. You sleep ok?'

'I think so.'

'Well, you went kinda strange. For a while, you wanted to go sleep in this baobab tree. Right up there at the top.'

I suddenly notice a good part of the bougainvillea has been ripped from the wall of the house. What's left of it hangs limply on the ground.

'Oh bugger!' I exclaim. 'I thought it was a dream. I'm very sorry, JP. I'll put the bougainvillea back.'

'Ah, what the hell,' JP draws in a deep breath. 'It sure is a great day to go fishing.'

THE SPORT-FISHING BOAT bobs in the waves, and a plume of water rises from the motor's propeller. The beach, the baobabs, the small palms, JP's white house and his ice station up on the escarpment all fade beyond the tumbling waves. We sit in our swivel chairs and watch it go. Yellowman, standing in the cabin and holding the steering wheel, stares ahead intently. Every so often, he turns his head to shout instructions to his assistant sitting at the stern of the boat, next to where the outboard motor is attached to the transom. When Yellowman shouts, the assistant makes fine adjustments to the angle of the motor with his outstretched bare foot, and in this manner, we negotiate our way through the shallow reef, where the surging waves explode white against the rocks, and we cross into the open sea.

Under Yellowman's guidance, the assistant steers the boat to a cluster of pirogues bobbing at anchor. The fishermen are huddled together in their boats, watching the sea, willing the fish onto their lines. The assistant meanders to the bow, removes the anchor from its stowage and throws it into the water. Then he gathers the rods and fixes the hooks and weights. He baits them with small fish and passes them to JP and me, and we cast the lines into the water. Yellowman cuts the motor and proceeds to strip the steering connection behind the wheel, until soon he has a collection of parts strewn across the deck. JP jigs his line slowly. Sucking on his pipe, he watches Yellowman studying the parts he's strewn about the deck.

'That pivot looks a bit dry,' he says. 'I've got some grease back in the house. You should've told me you had a problem.'

'Bin like this for a week.'

'Sure it has. You should've told me.'

We bob on the waves, talking about fishing for barracuda. Yellowman tells us about the old German who owns the boat and who likes to come out and fish with his wife.

'The wife is a better fisherman than the old German,' he tells us.

We debate for a while whether the German's wife would be a fisherman or a fisherwoman, and then my rod bows and jerks in my hands. I reel in the line, and we land a good-sized but ugly catfish. I reset the gear, and, in the distance, we catch sight of a huge dark form surfacing momentarily in the trough of a wave. We're undecided what it could be. Nobody's seen a whale here for a long time.

Yellowman painstakingly reassembles the steering control. JP sits in his swivel chair with his feet against the transom, playing the fishing rod in his hand. With the pipe clamped between his teeth, he and Yellowman discuss control looms, bearings, flanges, lubricating oils and suitable wires and their attendant connections. Relaxing here, JP appears to have not a care in the world, and I ponder what it is that makes him seek opportunity in a place like this. To a large degree, he is right when he says it depends on what one wishes to achieve, and the pressure we impose on ourselves to achieve it. And, perhaps, in Africa, identifying opportunity requires a large slice of imagination – which JP has in spades. For now, I strongly suspect it just suits him to be here. He is nomadic, after all. A wanderer doesn't need much stability in a place, only a reason to move on when the time is right. Perhaps his greatest aspiration is simply the freedom to move on. He might lose his ice station, his nice house on the beach and possibly all his engines, but he would certainly survive that. Some people spend a lifetime just wishing for the opportunity to move on.

When the fishermen chug to another position in the bay, Yellowman suggests we do the same. We follow this pattern most of the afternoon. We catch more catfish and a moray eel, which curls its long body and snaps its jaws, until the assistant hits it over the head with an iron bar and leaves it next to the outboard motor. After a while, it recovers and slips over the side.

We stop fishing not long after that and head to shore. Yellowman sets the engine speed and takes his turn on the transom, steering the outboard motor with his hands. He occasionally peers over the side to check his route. The steering still doesn't work, even after he's taken it all to pieces and put it back together again. It seems Yellowman is a better fisherman than a mechanic.

By late afternoon, Ousman arrives in his Land Rover, and we all head off to the airport. Musa comes with us for the ride.

'I see man on beach has gone now,' says JP.

'Finally, he catches the big fish,' Musa tells him. 'He comes to the station for ice, and I gave him some from the container. He is a nice man. He knows my uncle in Banjul.'

'Why he go fish with binoculars, this man who knows your uncle?'

'He just retired from the telephone company. They gave him binoculars as a present for very good service. He takes them everywhere. They are a very nice present.'

'Is that right?'

'I looked through them myself.'

'I bet you did.'

At the airport, we say our goodbyes.

JP claps me on the back. 'Don't leave it so long next time.'

'I won't. Just give me time to recover from this one.'

I check in my bag, and at immigration I fill out a long form which is stamped and placed in a drawer with a lot of crumpled paper. I go and sit on a metal chair in the departure hall and pull a book from my bag. The flight is delayed by two hours. For some reason, this airline prefers a schedule that runs two hours late. It might be easier for everyone if they adjusted their timetable.

'I've been looking for you!'

I start at the booming voice, and the book I'm reading drops from my hand in a mass of flapping pages.

When I look up, I'm staring into the face of Mohammed, the Commander of the National Intelligence Agency. Today, he's decked out in flowing white robes, and he's making a bit too much of a habit of creeping up on me. Is this all they taught him in spy school?

Then a shudder of fear strikes me – maybe they already

raided JP's house, uncovering his bag of African herbs? Is this a bust?

I do my best to mask the tremble in my hand as I recover the fallen book.

'How are you?' I ask.

'I am well. Come with me, please.'

I cast a look about me for the men in suits. I register only the tanned faces of the holidaymakers on their way home. Some of them eye me when I gather my things and follow Mohammed through a glass door into the sunshine. He indicates for me to sit at a table on the terrace in the shadow of a large, green sunshade and orders us both a drink. While we wait for our drinks, he regales me with stories of African politics and corruption, and the aftermath of colonial rule and its destabilising effect on Africa. Then he speaks of the rebels pushing north across the border from Senegal, and the devastation it will bring.

The waiter brings two bottles of soda, and while I pay, Mohammed is turning in his chair, scanning the other passengers on the terrace.

'Excuse me,' he booms at a man two tables from us. 'I must have that book if you finish it before you go. It is a very good book, no?' 'If I finish it in time, you may have it,' the man assures him. Mohammed turns back to me. 'That is a very good book. It is about a drug smuggler who managed to evade many of the world's top security agencies. Indeed, he worked in cahoots with some of them. Perhaps as a spy. He was a most unlikely criminal, I think. I would like to read this book. They caught him in the end, of course. You know, I spent many years working in London with MI5. And then with the FBI, in the United States. Always stay one step ahead of the criminals, they used to say to us. Use any means at your disposal to trap your target. But it's not always easy to keep one step ahead. We need eyes in the back of our heads.'

Mohammed picks up his soda and sucks from the straw. With a loud gurgle, the bottle is emptied before I've pocketed my wallet. Air rasps up the straw as he chases the last drops. He puts the bottle back on the table and burps into his hand.

'How is your pipe?' I ask. Mohammed's face is a complete blank. Suddenly, it lights up. 'Ah, yes. The pipe. Yes. It smokes very well.' His eyes come together as he leans closer to the table. 'JP is a good man, isn't he? People like him are good for Africa, don't you think?' 'I think he's very courageous to come here alone and do what he's doing with his ice station.' 'Courageous. Absolutely.' He works his head up and down in agreement. 'Well, I am very pleased you had a good trip, but now I must go. I have a flight coming in that I need to meet.' He rises to his feet and clamps my hand. 'Have a good journey back to England. And don't forget,' he winks at me with a cunning expression, 'come fishing again with Yellowman.'

I begin to wonder how many spies Mohammed has. I watch the Commander of the National Intelligence Agency stride across the terrace. He vanishes behind the reflective glass door, and I ponder whether Mohammed is a genuinely friendly man, or just trying to keep one step ahead.

7

THE FASTIDIOUS MR PETERS

It was the guy with the makeshift axe who particularly unnerved me. The way he raised it over his shoulder, ready to strike. The other fellow was drawing a roughly hewn arrow in his bow. We hadn't a clue where they'd sprung from, out here, in the middle of nowhere, among all the scrub and parched trees, beside this tomb crowned with zebu horns. We should not have taken a photo of the tomb, they cried. But now that we have, we must pay. It wasn't clear in what currency.

'We must retreat immediately to the motor car,' our guide advised.

That had seemed a good idea. To his credit, the guide spoke quietly and calmly to our two aggressors, while we slipped into the back seat of the van. Just as I was about to slide the door closed, the axeman lunged forward, grabbing my bag, spittle punctuating his fiery rhetoric. There was no reasoning with him. The guide shoved the door onto his arm, and when his hand darted back through the narrow gap, minus the bag, I slammed the door closed. The driver stamped on the accelerator, showering the two ruffians in a hail of dust and stones.

'Those were not nice men,' the guide declared, running a hand over his brow. 'I am sorry for this.'

This next story, geographically speaking, is a slight departure from the African continent. Madagascar is an island lying off the south-eastern coast of Africa, having broken away during the Early Jurassic period, about one hundred and eighty million years ago. It is steeped in mythology, and, to a good many, the dead and the place they are laid to rest are central to their lives, as we were quickly learning.

Later that same day, we'd been taking coffee at a village bar when an animated crowd passed through.

'Come,' said our guide, 'we shall follow them.'

Tagging on to the end of the line, we crossed several small fields, before reaching a large earth mound where a number of tombs adorned with zebu horns stood. After our earlier encounter with tombs and horns, I was still harbouring a little disquiet about this latest jaunt.

'Now you will witness the Famadihana,' the guide announced gleefully.

I felt uncomfortable being there, except they were demonstrably happy to have us join in with whatever it was they were about to do in this grand graveyard. Unlike the fury we unleashed in the axeman and his sidekick, on this occasion, taking photos was positively encouraged.

As one might expect in a country straining to get along, there are numerous Western aid agencies doing a great deal of good work. During our visit, I heard a wonderful tale of how aid destined for a particular project was diverted by the local administration to another cause equally close to their hearts. Though both parties seemed to be working toward the same goal, due to the recipients' vastly different culture and beliefs, they disagreed with the donor on how the particular problem should be tackled. No doubt, some busybody auditor could have instantly started wagging the finger. But was this really a cut and dried case of fraud, or a simple matter of ignorance?

The Fastidious Mr Peters is based on that account.

FRIDAY IS MARKET day in Avenue de l'Indépendance.

From his hotel balcony, Mr Peters looks down on the column of coloured parasols plugging the avenue, catching an occasional glimpse of the human hoard drifting beneath the gaps in the irregular canopy. He leans on the railing, his nose twitching at the heady mix of spices, rotting garbage and vehicle exhaust. And the noise – the irregular hum of voices, the clatter of construction work, the honking of car horns, the screech and squawk of animals, the shrieking of stall holders – oh yes, the noise is boundless.

He retreats into the room, shutting the door. Not that it's capable of blotting out the clamour. It's incapable of that because the door, in places, barely matches the frame. A barking dog and what Mr Peters can only imagine to have been a madman were with him most of the night, the fellow's gut-wrenching screams filling the room, competing with the high-pitched yelping. His only hope is that the door ajar holds the heat at bay.

He mollifies himself with the knowledge that Finar will soon be here. Together they will travel up-country to the rice paddies, where Mr Peters can observe first-hand how the three hundred thousand dollars donated by the All-

African Development Bank in London (better known in consultancy circles as the AADB) has been spent.

That's why Mr Peters is in Madagascar, to fulfil his role as auditor. To take photographs of the project and speak to the people concerned. To understand how their lives have been immeasurably improved by the generous grant to their project, the Central Highlands Rural Irrigation Scheme. He is here to witness their abundant rice crop and then report back to his superiors. For an independent consultant, particularly one not so long out of university, it is vital to cultivate a good reputation with the bank. Then, he may look forward to a promising career.

He goes to the rickety desk to check his things for the umpteenth time that morning. He can be quite fastidious when the moment warrants. His things are laid in a neat row, like troops on parade: the Dictaphone, the camera (with spare film), sunglasses, a wallet full of pens, a black notebook, the bank's questionnaire, a penknife and a small French-English dictionary. He lifts his canvas case from the floor, carefully putting all the objects inside. He keeps hold of the black notebook, taking a seat while he waits. The chair wobbles as he thumbs through the pages. When he comes to the briefing notes he'd made at the meeting in London with Mr Arthur J. Walters, head of rural affairs at the AADB, he pauses to read.

'Madagascar's an unusual place,' the head of rural affairs had pronounced while pulling wistfully on his tie. 'A place where rituals and taboos regulate much of their life. It's one of the world's poorest nations.' As Mr Peters reads his notes, all rather disjointed, as was the briefing he'd received, he recalls Mr Arthur J. Walters nodding sagely. 'The bank's help will be so greatly appreciated by the people. They are no longer self-sufficient in rice, you see, their main staple.

Anything we can do to alleviate such a situation can only be for the good. They have the highest per capita rice consumption in the world.' He went on to explain how their exports of coffee, cloves and vanilla did little to shore up the crumbling economy.

Walters had slid a briefing note across the table entitled – Madagascar: Its People and Culture. There were several crisp sheets of paper, stapled and, by the look of them, never before read.

'There are eighteen tribes. You'll be dealing mainly with the Merina. The capital city and the central highlands are principally their fiefdom.'

Mr Peters' fingers had ached with the speed at which he'd scribbled. Now, as he thumbs through the pages, he finds some of his writing utterly unintelligible. He flicks a page or two, until coming to the most unusual section of his briefing, the discussion concerning the various beasts that are rumoured to be prevalent in these parts. Quite what relevance this held for Mr Peters' report, he remains unsure. At least Mr Arthur J. Walters had slowed his pace by then. For a moment, the man had gazed at the ceiling, twirling the edge of his moustache between thumb and forefinger, his eyes a little demonic – an appearance, Mr Peters had thought, quite out of character for a banker. Not at all what he would have expected from the head of rural affairs.

'The Vazimba are a long-vanished pygmy tribe that haunt the landscape. And the Kalanoro, wild men of the woods, eat nothing but fruit and crabs.' Mr Peters recollects the skin reddening above his boss's moustache as he'd tugged harder, evidently warming to his subject. 'The Fanany is a snake-like animal with seven horned heads. And the Songomby, an ox-like creature moving like the wind, eating only warm human flesh.'

Mr Peters turns over the page of his notebook to find others, such as the Kinoly and the Angatra. He could have filled the whole book with such fanciful talk, for there seemed a considerable depth to the subject and his client's knowledge limitless.

As he closes the notebook now, one last piece of advice is ringing in his subconscious. It has to do with a taboo, or *fady*, which makes it unwise to sit in the doorway of a house while the rice is sprouting in the field, since the doorway of the house is compared to the gateway to life. By blocking it, one might impede the birth of the rice.

'It would be wise to garner at least a working knowledge of the *fady*,' Mr Walters advised. And with that, he'd ushered Mr Peters from the room and out into a damp London street.

Such a comprehensive brief had, on balance, left him as awed as he was informed. Though Mr Peters is not much given to an irresolute mind, for the sake of good order, he has consigned such fairy tales to a dim corner of his subconscious. There is, after all, a job to be done.

A light rap sounds at the bedroom door, and with such firmness of mind, he rises to draw it open.

'Good morning, Mr Peters.' Finar is smiling, though he looks no less anxious than the previous afternoon when they'd met at the airport. Mr Peters concludes, right there and then, that it is perhaps a look he's borne all of his life. Maybe the mere shock of arriving in such a place of complex beliefs and myth has placed an untold burden on Finar's sensitive soul.

'Did you sleep well, Mr Peters?'

'Marginally well.' For the moment, he sets aside all the noise and the attempt by someone, at two thirty-five in the morning, to enter his room. There seems little point burdening Finar with such matters. 'I should say it was better than the aeroplane, at least.'

Finar cocks his head to one side. 'Are they not so very comfortable, aeroplanes?'

'Not so much. I think one might term them a necessary evil. Shall we go?'

Mr Peters grabs his canvas case and sets the panama hat on his head. He closes the door, pursuing Finar down the stairs. 'You know, Finar, you really must call me Robert.'

'Yes, Mr Robert.'

Outside, it is oppressively hot. A clammy, dirty heat. Mr Peters grips the canvas case as they walk beneath the overhang of the building, along the edge of chaos, weaving between the jostling throng. He's never liked crowds at the best of times, and this is as damn near a rabble as he's ever encountered. He registers the multiple faces, the coffee-coloured complexion of the Malay or Indonesian ancestry, and the darker, heavier-featured Africans. This, he has already concluded, is where the Far East meets Africa, and a place where time has little influence.

In the narrow street leading from the avenue, a battered Citroën awaits them. Finar opens the back door for Mr Peters to climb aboard, and he slides onto the cracked leather seat. Finar hops into the front, pulling the door closed with a solid thud.

The driver turns to face him, and Mr Peters raises his panama, running a handkerchief over his damp brow. He nods at the driver, fearing he appears a little less urbane than he might have wished.

'Bonjour, Monsieur,' Mr Peters says.

'Bonjour, Monsieur,' the driver replies.

The driver starts the engine and the car's suspension lifts them gently into the air. He pulls away from the curb, the shifting wall of people gradually parting. They swerve around a rickety wooden cart. A wheel has slipped from the cart's axle and its contents now fill the gutter. A man and child in ragged clothes hold the wheel between them, and, as they pass them by, Mr Peters is conscious of their hooded eyes seeking him out.

'The journey will be about one hour,' Finar announces.

The tyres hum on the cobbled street, occasionally thudding as a wheel drops into a deep pothole. Mr Peters sits back, watching the city unfold, quietly thankful for the thoroughness of French suspension.

After an hour, they pass a large billboard – The Central Highlands Rural Irrigation Scheme. He sees the bank's name in the bottom right corner as they flash by and senses a flutter of excitement, briefly contemplating a photograph. It might look rather appropriate on the front of his report.

'Are we close now?'

Finar's head jolts upright, turning from side to side. 'Yes,' he says sleepily. 'Very close now.'

All around them are terraced paddy fields. Mr Peters' excitement is heightened by what he sees, his palms mildly damp as he rubs them together. Oh yes, he muses. I shall do a very nice report for the AADB, of that I am certain. I can feel it in my water.

On closer inspection, at least what is feasible from the moving car, he begins to worry that some of the terraces appear quite barren of not only people but, more alarmingly, crops.

'Where are all the people?'

Finar clears his throat. It's a low, rumbling noise that draws on for some moments. 'Today is a celebration. A Famadihana. They will not work on such a day.'

Mr Peters feels a tad unsettled. He doesn't wish to have

to return tomorrow. Tomorrow has been set aside for fleshing out the structure of his report. 'I need to interview the people. See the workings of the project.' He didn't mean to sound quite so curt.

'I'm sure they will be very happy to receive you, Mr Robert.'

They arrive at the entrance to a village. At least, that's how he can best describe the gathering of improvised shelters nestling among the crumbling colonial villas. The driver stops the car adjacent to what had once been a particularly ornate property. A balcony runs the length of the first floor, crumbling in parts, and an elaborate iron balustrade lines its edge. The paintwork is bleached and flaking. 'Chez Marie' is barely visible on the sign above the door.

Finar is facing him. 'We have a little time. Perhaps you wish to take a coffee?'

'That would be nice.'

It is a place he will not forget in a hurry. Inside, the wooden floor is dark, like the room itself, and the boards spring and creak as they cross them. A significant glass chandelier hangs in the centre, the baubles reflecting what scarce sunlight finds its way between thick curtains. Dust spirals in the shafts of light, and Mr Peters considers that if he were to take the pocket knife from the canvas case, he could most likely cut the must and general decay flourishing in the place.

They settle at a table with wrought-iron legs and a wooden top. Even in the gloom, he can see the walls are lined with a fine burgundy and gold material, most probably silk, he thinks.

The room undoubtedly has presence. Mr Peters admits that he's not much blessed with imagination, yet even he senses the elegance that must have once occupied the space between these walls. It has been captured in the décor. Though not as visible as the dust, it is equally present.

Finar orders two coffees from a shadow lingering by an inner door, and in due course, they arrive.

For now, Mr Peters is unsure whether it is in the details he notes down that will make Chez Marie stick in his mind, or if it has more to do with the ominous sense of foreboding. The feeling of things not quite going to plan.

'Mr Robert.' Finar toys with his coffee cup. His hand slips, and coffee sloshes into the saucer. 'There are some things about the Malagasy people I must tell you, so that you may at least understand them a little better.'

Mr Peters is certain, after what he's learnt back in London, that he's duly prepared for anything Finar discloses. He listens attentively all the same.

Finar rotates the cup in the saucer a fraction at a time when he says, 'Can you for a moment – just for today, I mean – can you imagine the most important, the most influential people in your family being the deceased?'

Mr Peters is suddenly conscious of his open mouth. He closes it hurriedly.

'You see... what I'm trying to explain is, the spirits of the razan, our ancestors, they are of greater consequence than the living. Without their guidance, we are unable to function. We are with them all of the time, you see, as surely as if they walk by our side in the fields. A family will live all its life in poverty to ensure the spirits of their ancestors enjoy comfort and standing in the spirit world, for it is only in such a way, it is only when a spirit is revered by the living, that it can truly be an influence in the spirit world. They act as intermediaries between God and humankind and will influence the good fortune, or otherwise, of their family. It is not enough for an ancestor to be laid beneath the ground.

He must have the finest tomb the family can buy. He must be wrapped in the finest cloth and, as a sign of his wealth and standing, all the zebu that he owns must be slaughtered and feasted upon, their skulls placed upon the tomb.

'Today is the ceremony of the Famadihana, the turning of the bones. It is a time of togetherness. A time when we can be with our ancestors. I'm sure you will understand better after you have experienced it.'

Finar smiles, though his forehead is still deeply furrowed.

Mr Peters is about to respond, for a terrible thought is taking root, soon to be dashed by a chanting outside. The din becomes louder, accompanied by the regular thudding of a drum. It is coming from somewhere beyond these heavy curtains.

Too soon, Mr Peters finds himself carried along by it, drawn from the sombre Chez Marie and into the bright sunlight. Outside, a colourful procession snakes up the road and down a narrow path running between the fields. He can see now where they are heading, to a hillock not so very far away, to where the walls of a rather grand tomb rise from the crest. Even from this distance, he can make out the horns of the many zebu that adorn it, like a fortification of thorn scrub.

'Come.' Finar beckons to him. 'It is time for us to go to the land of the ancestors.'

Mr Peters adjusts the panama over his head, and they merge into the procession.

Now he's closer to the fields, he can see how badly the rice crop has taken. In places, the earth is simply a web of parched cracks. But why has the irrigation scheme failed so utterly? He doesn't like what he sees in the least, and neither, he suspects, will his client.

It takes an age for the people to finally assemble. Mr Peters holds back a respectful distance yet wishing only to crack on with his findings. And yet he knows there is nothing to be done at this moment. His timing is quite appalling. He scans the mass of gathered faces, wondering who might enlighten him as to what has happened to the crop. Who might be the one? He wants to ask Finar so that, unbeknownst to them, he can at least begin to assess their character from a distance. To gain a modicum of advantage.

At the front of the tomb, an old man begins speaking. His voice carries strongly despite his visible frailty. Behind him, men mingle by the magnificent tomb.

Mr Peters feels Finar at his shoulder. 'This is the Mpanandro. He is like a magic man. Now they will begin opening the tomb, the first time in five years.'

It is the most unusual ceremony Mr Peters has ever clapped eyes on. One by one, the ancestors, wrapped in silk cloth, are withdrawn from the lower chamber of the tomb. They are placed on the ground, and the remains transferred to a new silk shroud, while hushed words are exchanged between the living and the spirits of their loved ones. With the new shrouds in place, half a dozen relatives hold each one aloft, the swaying of their bodies accompanied by a brief song. With the ceremony completed, the ancestors are once again returned to the tomb.

'Perhaps now you can understand a little better the bond between the living and the dead.' Finar holds out his hands toward the tomb. 'And the respect they bestow upon the razan. Such respect will be rewarded in everything mankind does.'

'Oh, yes!' Mr Peters finds himself saying. 'Having seen such a ceremony, I understand completely what you mean.'

Most people have left the hillock, with only a few stragglers remaining. Mr Peters is itching to commence the interviews. He scuffs the parched ground with the toe of his shoe. 'The bank is keen to learn how their money has helped the community, Finar. To understand where the funding has been spent. Maybe we should start with the infrastructure.'

'Ah, yes... the infrastructure,' Finar repeats. He saunters forward, going to stand beside the tomb, where he raps his knuckles against the solid stonework. 'You see all these beautiful new tombs we've built, Mr Robert. Now we will have a wonderful harvest.'

Mr Peters' shoulders sag, and he shakes his head despondently. With a sense of dread, he removes the camera from his canvas case.

'You better smile,' he instructs Finar. Because he's certain Mr Arthur J. Walters will not.

8

NOTES FROM A SOUTHERN-AFRICA SAFARI

2009 KwaZulu-Natal, South Africa.

It's a precarious beginning. A snake in the shower is rarely a joyous start to the new day, especially when it's one of the continent's most venomous.

Condensation coats the interior of the tent, and I lie here a moment in the calm before the storm, breathing the humid air, eyeing a quivering bead of water directly above me. Throwing off the bedclothes, I unzip the flap, peering outside. A mist has rolled in overnight, concealing the wetlands surrounding us, a heavy dew causing the greenery to weep drops of moisture. There's a rhythmic tapping as they tumble from leaf to leaf, the drops forging small indents in the sand.

There is only one other client in this camp, a South African family who left in the early hours to go on a fishing trip. Their white Toyota pokes from an abundance of stone-coloured canvas, various camping paraphernalia scattered around. A thin trail of smoke rises from a grey fire. Two young men tasked with guarding the South Africans' equipment slump in chairs, blankets gripped about their shoulders. They look miserable. When I wave, one of them returns the gesture, though he is quick to snatch the blanket threatening to unfurl from his shoulder.

The first shriek breaks the stillness as I descend the ladder from Kubu's (Kubu is our trusty pickup) rooftop tent. It comes from the ablution block. I know who it is. With one foot on the ground, I throw a look at the two guards. A second shriek is followed by a short interval of silence, after which Christine bursts into sight, hastily winding the towel around her torso.

'There's a snake in my shower,' she cries.

He's fast, I'll give him that. Barely had the blanket touched the ground, and the guard was on his feet, a rock already in his hand.

'Don't kill it,' she calls after him as he vanishes into the building.

A minute later, he reappears.

'It's gone now,' he says, though he doesn't say where to. 'It was a green mamba. Not a good snake to shower with.'

I'm not a fan of snakes, harbouring, as I do, a morbid fascination for their ability to incapacitate. To kill. For a human, the venom from a green mamba is often fatal. One has to know these things. He was right, the guard: not a good showering partner.

'It was enormous,' Christine says.

'Madam. That was just the baby. The mother will be here somewhere.'

LATER, Abraham, our local guide, takes us for a walk through the wetland and to help us find someone who might sell us fish we can cook on the fire. We come across a cheerful fellow called Moses, knee-deep in one of the salt water lakes, a spear in his right hand. He strides ashore to show us the several mullet shimmering inside a cloth bag hanging from his shoulder.

'You caught all these with the spear?'

'Oh, yes,' he says.

We offer to buy one, but he won't have it.

'This mullet is a gift for you,' he says, pulling one of the fish from the bag. 'I'm very happy to see you in my country.'

Moses has a very nice car parked in the shade, and when he sees me admiring it, he declares, 'I work in the forestry sector.' They must pay well in the forestry sector, I surmise. His wife, his brother's wife, and several of their friends wave at us from the shade beside the car.

Moses wraps one of the fish in a sheet of newspaper and hands it to me.

'I love to catch fish the old way,' he says, holding his spear proudly. 'Now we are going to have a braai. I will cook these fish for my family and friends.'

After saying goodbye to Moses and his family, Abraham leads us through the bush back to camp, which takes us one and a half hours, and then we cook Moses' fish on an open fire, just as he'd told us we should. It tastes delicious.

Mozambique

The following morning, we drive to the Kosi Bay-Ponta do Ouro international border and cross into Mozambique. It's a Sunday, and it's quiet, the formalities on both sides proceeding smoothly. For the first thirty kilometres after the border, we follow a track cutting through low dunes. For the purposes of navigation, we supplement our common sense by using an old, trusted Garmin GPS that simply offers us a heading for Bela Vista. It's a kind of 'as-the-crow-flies' navigation, perfect if you're in an airplane, or a boat on the open sea. The track we follow through the dunes splits on various occasions, leaving us to meander up the coast towards Maputo, the capital of Mozambique, with at one moment Bela Vista featuring some way beyond the left side of the pickup and, at other times, somewhere on the right.

Finally, we find the laterite road and can increase our speed. There are no campsites out here, and being uncertain about the security situation, we press on for Maputo, finding Maputo Backpackers, a hostel on the coast road to Costa do Sol. We cross the city to get there; it is not impressive to look at – a preponderance of grim, concrete shells. The infrastructure has been devastated by the civil war, so a lot of construction work is taking place. Its saving grace is a most imposing central railway station.

This evening, we choose to dine at an old Maputo establishment, Restaurant Costa do Sol, famous for its seafood. Seduced by the white beach, we take advantage of the last of the light to amble up the coast towards the restaurant. Halfway there, we begin to wish we hadn't, for no other reason than this city has a bad reputation for violent crime. At all the fuel stations we've passed in Maputo, guards with AK-47s patrol the forecourts. During the night, the dogs never cease their barking.

Leaving grey Maputo behind us, we arrive at Chidenguele and the Sunset Beach Lodge, seizing a late morning beer on the wooden deck overlooking white sands and the Indian

Ocean. They charge two hundred metical for two nights on their campsite. What the Sunset Beach lacks in palm trees was adequately compensated for by the Morrungulo Beach Resort at Inhambane. We laze under the willowy palms as spear fishermen patrol the beach selling lobsters.

GORONGOSA NATIONAL PARK was at one time Renamo's HQ during the civil war, until they were driven out in 1992. From 1977 to 1992, the conflict was principally fought between Mozambique's ruling Marxist Mozambique Liberation Front (Frelimo) and the anti-communist insurgent forces of the Mozambican National Resistance (Renamo). During the 70s, this park was one of Africa's most prolific game reserves, until becoming Renamo's larder.

For the first hour, we forge our way along tracks cutting through thick bush. This is no time to worry about Kubu's paintwork. Only 15 per cent of the park's four thousand square kilometres of grassland, forest and mountain terrain is accessible by car. We finally break out onto a plain. To the north, the view of Gorongosa Mountain rising to eighteen hundred metres altitude and, in the foreground, a mass of plains game – kudu, impala, waterbuck, duiker and many, many warthogs. A truly magnificent sight. We take out our chairs, make coffee and seize the moment.

Later, we find the old Lion House, formerly a camp building, now abandoned and ruined. Sometimes there are lions here on the roof, scanning the plain for prey. With the financial assistance of the Carr Foundation, hopefully this park will return to its former glory.

It feels good to finally get off the beaten track in Mozambique. There have been so many warnings not to stray into the more remote regions for fear of the land mines and live ordnance that remains scattered throughout the country.

Malawi

Ernest is the chief ranger of Liwonde National Park, and he's very keen for me to understand that he has an M16 assault rifle in his arsenal of weaponry. Perhaps he thinks I look a bit shifty. Inside the building, at the park entrance, where we go to pay our entry fee, he points to several old carbines lying clustered together on the floor of his office.

'Those are for my men,' he says.

Mvuu Camp is twenty-eight kilometres from the park entrance, and there, the monkeys have taken stealing the campers' food to an art form. While the vervets scurry back and forth like a troop of racketeers, the *capo di tutti capi* is undoubtedly the baboon. With a few well-thrown sticks, I've pretty much got the measure of these ruffians. That is until I make the error of leaving one of the passenger doors open.

'Can you fetch the eggs we bought in Zomba,' Christine asks, preparing an omelette at the back of the vehicle. 'They're on the backseat of the car.'

With half a mind on the job, I pitch forward into the back of the pickup, only to be confronted by a baboon the size of a heavyweight wrestler, egg yolk dribbling over his chin. I recoil in horror.

'Get out,' I shriek most impotently.

Settled amidst the detritus on Kubu's backseat, he simply turns his head and flashes dripping fangs. This baboon is going nowhere until that carton of eggs in his lap is finished.

. . .

AT MZUZU, we follow the road to Chintheche, which runs through lush hilly country, eventually descending to the Chintheche Lodge beside Lake Malawi. It's quiet here, and finally, we have a shower offering hot water. We spend some time talking with Charles, the watchman for the lodge and its grounds. His given name is Lusungu, a Tumbuka name. He is an ace goalkeeper. Or so he says.

While I do the washing after dinner, Charles tells me without a hint of mirth that, in Africa, it is illegal for a man to wash dishes.

'Only the women do the cooking and the washing,' he says. The men work in the fields.

I tell him I've seen plenty of women working in the fields. Probably more women than men, come to think of it. He ignores such observations, simply pointing to a mural on the wall of the lodge depicting an African woman doing the washing up.

'This was painted by Duncan,' he informs us. 'In 1999.'

Apparently, Duncan made good money from his art, after which he spent it all on beer and womanising.

'He was dead at thirty,' Charles declares. 'From AIDS.'

While Charles cooks a fish on our fire, he tells us we mustn't venture up to Mount Mulanje after dark, for the Shadow Witch who lives up there in the mist-shrouded woodlands may curse us. He says he knows people who have heard her cackle in the night and is much relieved to hear we are not going there. He puts the cooked fish in his trouser pocket for later, recovering a slice of cassava from the same pocket. He tells us we should try it. I pick the fluff from it and break it in two, giving a piece to Christine. It is tasteless and not unlike the baobab fruit, though much less nutritious.

When Charles leaves at ten o'clock in the evening, he releases two hounds over which neither he nor anybody else at the property appears to have any control.

'How do we get to the bathroom now?' we ask him.

'Don't worry,' he says. 'These dogs don't attack white people.'

The next day, he brings Julius Longwe to see us. It's fifteen years since we last met Mr Longwe on this beach. He was a teacher back then, at the Chihame Full Primary School and has since taken retirement. Mr Longwe thanks us for all the football shirts we've provided the children over the years, though he admits this has caused some problems of jealousy with the other teachers. His wife has died since we last met, and now he has a younger one, with whom he has had four more children. His two albino kids are being educated at a private school, costing him twenty thousand kwacha a term, and his monthly pension is only fifteen thousand kwacha. His house, which he had first started building when we last met him, is almost finished.

'What can you do for me?' he asks, munching on a Digestive biscuit and sipping his mug of tea.

Christine gives him one of her shirts – a gift for his wife – and we write down his bank details.

AT CHITIMBA, the sign says fifteen kilometres to Livingstonia, and the road is very steep, twisty and broken. Near the top, the oil temperature warning light for the automatic gearbox begins to glow. On the way up, we collect a couple of backpackers, Maxime and Geoff, so we are a bit heavier when we reach the top. Passing a mushroom farm, we finally arrive at the Lukwe Eco Camp and share a pastis with our companions, watching the sun sink over the Rift Valley.

Livingstonia was founded in 1894 by missionaries of the Free Church of Scotland. It lies between Lake Malawi and the Nyika Plateau. At one thousand three hundred metres altitude, it is declared mosquito (and therefore malarial) free. It takes us one hour to walk there from our camp, and we find a peaceful village with a good feel to it. The buildings are made from brick, and there is a hospital supporting the region's inhabitants. Dr Robert Laws headed the missionary for more than fifty years, from 1878 until his retirement in 1927. Prior to moving to this location, the mission was originally sited at Cape Maclear, on the shores of the lake. However, this was considered an unhealthy location due to the prevalence of malaria. Dr Laws was brought up and educated in Aberdeen. The Stone House, where he used to live, now contains a museum detailing his and his colleagues' work.

It's amazing how Lake Malawi resembles a sea, with the waves breaking powerfully on the beach. And always this breeze. An eagle swoops in, snatching a fish from the water. On the far side lie the hills of Tanzania. Now almost at the top of the lake, we are eighty kilometres short of the border with Tanzania. Mark, who runs this camp, tells us how he used to breed rabbits here. Except, day after day, he kept finding the bunnies laid dead on the ground around camp, and he couldn't for the life of him work out why. After some time, he discovered one of the resident monkeys had taken to cuddling them. When he retired for the evening to the higher branches of the trees, the monkey would often take a bunny with him for company. Mark could only assume that when the monkey fell asleep he let go of the rabbit, and hence, they fell out of the tree.

Tanzania

The Ruaha National Park covers an area of more than twenty thousand square kilometres and is named after the Great Ruaha River, which flows through this ancient land. The entrance lies one hundred and thirty kilometres west of Iringa, at the end of a badly corrugated track.

What is extraordinary is how a herd of elephants can pass within twenty metres of our camp almost soundlessly. We stay close to the pickup until the last of them has moved out of sight. Though that's not to say they've moved off altogether, for the bush is thick here.

It is late afternoon now, the sun already descending, and we're not sure we've actually reached the designated campsite. There is no evidence of other campers having ever been here; the ground is littered with elephant and antelope dung; the long-drop latrine in the wooden structure is ripe and long-abandoned. What had been a waterway has baked dry, the earth shattered under the sun's glare. It's too late to move now, in any case. This will have to do.

The African night comes quickly. We take a bucket shower in the dying light, make a fire and debate the likely danger from predators. The buzzing of flies is replaced by the clicking of frogs, and a myriad moths flutter in the lantern's pool of light. Christine cooks a stew over the coals. 'There's no lions here, anyway,' she says.

Her timing is perfect. The first roar is closer to us than we might have wished for. This is immediately answered by a lion behind us, lurking in this wall of darkness. We exchange nervous glances, stoke the coals and place another piece of wood on the fire. Our principal lion-fighting weapon is a pepper spray with a two-metre range. This doesn't fill us with much comfort. Failing that, it's a knife and fork. Before long, the intensity and proximity of the calling cause us to retreat up the ladder to the rooftop tent, where we eat our supper and watch the firelight create the shifting shapes of lions from out of the shadows.

FOR ALL ITS HYPE, the Serengeti has proved a disappointment. We have been sent to Dik Dik Camp in the Seronera area of the park, and it is overflowing with tourist groups. The facilities are very poor for this number of people; by evening, we resemble a refugee camp with an expensive entry fee. Fortunately, we've secured a spot on the camp's perimeter and can enjoy a view across the plains to distant hills.

Today, we spot our first cheetah. It's lying in the shade of a tree, though raising your binoculars here in the Serengeti immediately attracts a procession of safari vehicles full of chattering tourists and, consequently, one's moment with Africa instantly evaporates. We head south-west to escape the crowds, and for a couple of hours, it is bliss, until a large herd of buffalo block further progress. There's no way we're going to attempt pushing through this sea of horns.

This evening, hyenas come scavenging in camp, their demonic howls sending a shiver down the spine. Stupidly, I've left our plastic jerry of water at the foot of the ladder and, in their frenzy to feed, they chew the handle clean off it. I'm glad we're up a ladder, and not in one of these canvas mushrooms on the ground.

All the game will be leaving for the Mara soon,

following their traditional migration north. Only, the rains have not come yet, meaning the grasses up there are poor.

We leave the park along the western corridor and head for Mwanza. At a garage on the way into town, a guy removes an impressive-looking bolt from one of Kubu's tyres that we've picked up from the track in the park. He patches the tyre, fits an inner tube, and we continue to the Tunza Lodge, beside Lake Tanganyika. We are tired, and our heads are full of dust. It is a moment to rest and to plan the next part of our journey. Jan and Nico, owners of the lodge, invite us to a braai. We're joined by their friend who works in a gold mine down in Geita. They discuss the live game trade, where a bull rhino costs as much as one hundred and fifty thousand US dollars. A male buffalo can set you back one hundred thousand US. At these prices, stocking a private reserve with game is no mean feat. After a good lunch, and a few too many Serengeti beers, Christine and I unfurl the map and make a brave decision.

We jostle to board the 10:30 a.m. ferry across the Mwanza Gulf. There is chaos among the buses and the people and the nauseating clouds of black exhaust. The road south proves hellish and is a portent of the journey to come. The road to Geita is under construction by the Chinese (as are so many roads in Africa) and, for some unexplainable reason, is covered in kilometre after kilometre of plastic sheeting; a temporary track of deep ruts and bull-dust weaves alongside it. The road skirts the southern border of Burundi, in the direction of Lake Tanganyika, and Jan has told us to beware of the refugees crossing over from the Congo. Some of them have turned to banditry.

The second night, we secure space at a United Nations compound, where a hefty gin and tonic eases the rigours of the drive. I wonder if the route we've decided upon is too remote, and I pray the road conditions might improve. We are mentally prepared for it to take us a week to follow the lake south, before finally reaching Kipili, our destination.

The next day, we leave at eight, refuel and get five hundred metres down the track to discover a truck jack-knifed in the deep sand. Dropping two wheels into the ditch beside the track, we eventually crawl past. Later, we squeeze past a road grader, precisely the type of vehicle that should be repairing this track and is instead transporting bunches of bananas.

During the coming days, the settlements become fewer, and the track ever worse – heavy corrugations, deep bull dust, rocks, potholes, craters, and all of it through a never-ending forest. Most of the way, we average twenty kilometres an hour in order to keep Kubu in one piece. The idea of a vehicle repair out here doesn't bear considering.

After Namanyere, we ascend and descend a low range of hills. The track is rocky. Kipili is close now, and due to these rocks, we resist the temptation to up the speed and hurry the journey's end. It has indeed taken us seven days to do approximately six hundred kilometres. But this drive has one more trick up its sleeve: with a bang like a pistol shot, one of our back tyres explodes. A sharp rock has punched a hole through it.

Chris and Louise are our hosts at the Lake Shore Lodge at Kipili, and upon arriving, we set up camp in the shade of a mango tree and immediately crack open a beer at the bar. A sundowner cruise out on the lake is followed by dinner in the restaurant. This is a wonderful place, and our six days of R&R pass like a dream.

Our seventh day is to be something of an adventure. Chris has been harbouring a plan to drive the quads to Katavi National Park, and while the distance is undetermined, he expects to achieve it in a day.

'What are the roads like?' I ask, to which I receive a puzzled stare.

'There are no roads,' Chris says.

We depart after breakfast at 7:30. Christine and I share one quad, while Chris and one of his staff, Agaard, drive the other two. We are loaded with water, extra fuel and one spare tyre. Such is Chris's confidence that we have only sufficient food for a lunchtime snack.

Before long, we leave behind the local settlements and vanish into the bush. Navigating with the aid of Chris's (very rudimentary) GPS, we are soon bridge building, river crossing and beating a track through the elephant grass. By mid-afternoon, we enter the Game Management Area bordering the national park and uncover a hideout for poachers, where cooked meat is laid on racks over the glowing coals, and beans bubble in a pot. Thinking we must be rangers, the poachers have scarpered, the tools of their trade – bows and arrows, wire snares, spears and knives – scattered about their camp. It's all rather sinister.

By nightfall, we cross an expanse of burnt forest, and the fading light forces us to stop. We are all physically exhausted; our food supply is finished, and only four litres of drinking water remain. Aside from that, we are completely lost.

While Agaard lights a fire, using my satellite phone, Chris makes contact with Louise and gives her our position. Having located us on Google Maps, she calls back five minutes later offering us a bearing to follow in the morning. With little else to do, we settle our bedding amongst the ashes and soot to grab whatever sleep we can. To his credit, Agaard keeps the fire going throughout the night; we are, after all, in big cat country. In the early hours, the tsetse fly bites I've suffered along the way begin to aggravate.

Rising early to make the most of the cool air, we head east through the burnt woodland on the bearing Louise has given us. A settlement called Kisi is our goal. After crossing more rough country, we finally break out on a track leading through the forest, following it until it brings us to a laterite road. This is our chance to open up the quads, and we soon arrive at a village south of Kisi, where we breakfast on a hearty potato omelette and a mug of coffee. Any further ideas of reaching Katavi National Park are instantly dismissed. A three-hour drive down the road returns us to the Lake Shore Lodge and a welcome opportunity to sluice away the soot.

That evening, over dinner, Chris tells me he has another expedition in mind, one which entails following a river from its source, all the way to Lake Tanganyika.

'It's rough country,' he admits. 'Though, I know someone who can bring a rifle.'

I hastily bow out.

A TARMAC ROAD runs through the centre of Sumbawanga. It's the only stretch of tarmac we've seen for the last five hundred kilometres. We take fuel, restock the larder and make for the Forest Way Country Club, an establishment owned by a Mr Amir K. Mitha. We meet Mr Mitha in the reception. Now most likely in his eighties, this club had once been his home. When his wife died nine years ago, and all his kids left, he turned the establishment into a hotel. At one time, he made his living as a game hunter in Katavi, offering his services to members of the British administration. He is a fervent believer in ghosts and juju, he confesses, his features lightening as he tells us the story of Mama Katavi and the legend of the village sinking into the earth.

'The village was replaced by a lake,' he says. 'And the hippos who live there have assumed the spirits of the people.'

At supper, we are served fish from the lake. After the waiter puts the plates in front of us, he hovers over the table, a steaming bowl in each hand.

'Chipsy or ricey?' he asks.

Zambia

We take turns driving for one hour each. We are back to averaging twenty kilometres an hour, and over the next one hundred and twenty-five kilometres, venture deeper and deeper into more remote country. We pass occupied villages, yet the track is devoid of other traffic. Every so often, the track collapses into deep holes, and the rocks are treacherous. By late afternoon, we clear the Tanzanian border control, though on the Zambian side, there are no officials, and the gate is padlocked. To get around the problem of the padlocked gate, I drive Kubu across a field, over a narrow bridge spanning a drainage ditch and arrive in Zambia.

The condition of the road to Mbala is as bad as anything we've encountered in Tanzania. We stay the night at Chila Lodge, beside Lake Chila, owned by a Mr Chala. 'Mr Chala of Chila' has a certain ring to it, I think. Being Saturday, the drinkers are in full swing, and the music is booming. Mr Chala tells us of a big battle between the British and the Germans during the First World War. When hostilities finished, all the guns were thrown in the lake, he says.

Lake Tanganyika was the scene of one of the strangest battles in the war. In their quest to capture Tanzania, formerly German East Africa, the allied forces had to control the lake. The Germans, however, dominated this huge expanse of water with the SMS *Graf von Goetzen* and two converted steamers. Because of this, the British could not successfully deploy their troops.

Big game hunter John Lee persuaded the British Admiralty that small motor gunboats, brought to the lake overland, could defeat the Germans. And so began a tale of British pluck and eccentricity. HMS *Mimi* and HMS *Toutou*, two forty-foot motor launches, were transferred from England by sea to South Africa and carried overland to Lake Tanganyika.

In the event, the British boats first knocked out the two steamers, and then sometime later, the SMS *Graf von Goetzen* was scuttled. Hoorah for British pluck!

The next day, we seek out an immigration officer, who sways and smells of alcohol. Our passports having been stamped into the country by an inebriated immigration officer, a forty-five-minute drive to Mpalanga takes us to the customs office, where we must temporarily import our vehicle. Like his immigration colleague, we find Mr Zimba in a bar and a little the worse for wear. He's quick to tell us the boss has the keys to the office, but he's gone to church. Hopefully, the boss will return from church sober. Come back later, Mr Zimba says.

Filling time doing chores, we go to the bank to withdraw cash from the ATM. The ATMs and the fuel stations have been a good measure of the state of security in each of the countries we've passed through. In South Africa, they were guarded by men wielding pump-action shotguns. In Mozambique, they had Kalashnikovs. In Tanzania, Bowie knives. Here in Zambia, a wizened-looking fellow perches on a wooden stool grasping a catapult.

At Shiwa Ngandu, we soak in the Kapishya hot springs. The lodge and campsite here are owned by Mark Harvey, grandson of the late Sir Stewart Gore-Browne. In 1920, Gore-Browne acquired twenty-five thousand acres of land in Northern Rhodesia, where he became the architect and creator of Shiwa House, an eccentric and magnificent manor house in which he could live his dreams of paradise. After visiting this extraordinary property, we stroll up the hill to Gore-Browne's burial site, enjoying the view over Lake Ishiba Ngandu, which, in the Bemba language, means 'lake of the royal crocodile'. This lake is said to have been visited by the famous Victorian missionary explorer Dr David Livingstone, who, at the time of his visit, lost his dog to one of the crocs.

In the afternoon, I make an oven out of abandoned bricks, in which Christine cooks a most excellent loaf of bread.

Reaching Lusaka, we take the pickup for a service, retiring to an Irish pub to enjoy a plate of fish and chips while we wait. Later, at Pioneer Camp, we meet a couple driving their vehicle round Africa.

'I'm worried,' the lady admits rather despairingly. 'I don't think Boris is going to make it much further.'

Oh dear! Not knowing the husband's name, I fear he must be gravely ill, even though he looks a decent colour. But that's not the case at all. The Boris she's referring to is their 4x4, and he's suffering from a cracked axle. They fuss around him as if he might be their child. I completely sympathise with their plight, having spent many kilometres fretting over how Kubu was holding up in some of these tough conditions. They're taking him to see the mechanic in the morning. We wish them luck.

From Lusaka, we follow the Great Western Road all the way to the entrance of Kafue National Park. When we arrive at McBride's Camp, Chris McBride is busily slotting shells the size of milk bottles into his Rigby 416 rifle to an audience of four Dutch girls, while simultaneously discussing the merits of lions on the health of an ecosystem.

'If you hear two or more lions roaring together in wild country,' he's saying, 'you know immediately that everything else is in good order.'

With that, he leads them into the bright sunlight, soon vanishing beyond the encroaching bush.

We meet Chris at 6:30 the next morning and, in the company of one of his scouts, head out to see what we might find. Chris slings the Rigby over his shoulder, though it appears too bulky for his angular frame. In his right hand, he carries a mug of coffee and tells us he's been up half the night reading *Alice in Wonderland*. Getting into his stride, he soon slips into a very good impression of Inspector Clouseau and for a while, we're mimicking our favourite scenes from the Pink Panther series. And that's before we reach the coffee cup tree.

'Have you ever seen a coffee cup tree?' he asks.

Five hundred metres out of camp, he stops, drains the mug of coffee and hangs if from the branch of a tree. There are another three mugs similarly dangling from the same tree.

'They'll come and get them eventually,' he says. 'When we've no mugs left in camp.'

Shortly, the scout spots the spoor of a big lion in the sand. Right on cue, a blood-chilling roar cuts through the woodland.

'It's probably The Phantom,' Chris chirps excitedly. 'You're very lucky,' he gushes. Right at that moment, I'm not sure I feel that lucky.

The Phantom is an enormous lion as yet unseen by Chris. We follow the spoor along the river, in the direction of where a lion is calling, until the scout sees a tail swishing back and forth. We stop dead. A lioness observes us from over the grasses and the scout whispers that the male is lying next to her, almost out of sight. He holds his hands out wide, indicating the size of its head. He's sure it's The Phantom, except no one wishes to go any closer to confirm it, so we retreat to a large anthill, where we slump against a fallen tree, sipping coffee and debating the usefulness of these tsetse flies, which are again attempting to bite us. Chris has an interesting viewpoint. As the farmers and pastoralists expand their land occupation, the tsetse fly provides the greatest defence for the national parks, for neither man nor their beasts can exist alongside it. They therefore provide the perfect natural barrier to human encroachment.

I can't argue against that, I tell him, slapping one off my leg.

Before long, Chris slips into a rendition of *The Goon Show*, a comical radio programme of the 1950s and '60s:

Peter Sellers – 'Here, take one of my business cards.'

Harry Secombe – 'Why, there's nothing on it.'

Peter Sellers – 'I must say. Business is a little blank at present.'

From McBride's Camp, we go south, re-entering the park after Itezhi-Tezhi. These are classic African plains of open grassland and mopane forest. The track, weaving through the grassland, is at one moment heavy sand and the next hard-packed dambo, or seasonal wetland. We see black smoke rising in our direction, and the raging fire sweeping the plain soon cuts the track ahead of us. With little idea of the fire's depth, we stop to consider our options. Turn back, or make a dash for it? We'll make a dash for it, we decide. Closing the windows, we accelerate towards the leaping flames. Just before we enter the blaze, I worry that somebody coming from the opposite direction has had the same idea. For what seems an eternity, we are cast into an inferno, the flames licking Kubu's paintwork. Soon enough, we are on the other side of it, each of us breathing a sigh of relief.

The following morning, we set out from Nanzhila Plains Safari Camp at first light. The temperature registers a cool ten degrees centigrade on Kubu's dash, yet by midday, it will again be oppressively hot. At the Chelenje Pools, we park beside a copse of trees, climb onto the roof with the camera and binoculars and wait. We've been told to come here by the guys at the lodge because, they say, we stand a good chance of sighting one of the world's most endangered species. And before too long, we are rewarded when a pack of African Wild Dogs, nine of them in all, come trotting in. This is a magical and privileged moment: just the two of us and these rare creatures, with their oversized ears and colourful, patchy coats. They drink at the pools before frolicking in the long grasses. Opportunistic predators that hunt medium-sized ruminants, the African Wild Dog (or African

Painted Dog) can reach speeds of seventy kilometres an hour.

The town of Livingstone, established in 1905, was named after Dr David Livingstone. Now a busy tourist centre, there is clearly a classic human-wildlife conflict in the making. As the town expands rapidly and the buildings and fences multiply, the local elephant population is increasingly denied its habitual movement between the feeding grounds and the river. As we approach the suburbs from the north, there's a herd of them here right now, attempting to negotiate this line of traffic shunting into town, with various drivers unhelpfully shouting at them, others hooting their horns. The elephants are agitated, trumpeting and flapping their ears, and soon enough, something or someone is going to be broken.

Ahead of us, a line of mist hangs in the air – Mosi-oa-Tunya – 'the smoke that thunders'. It is here at Victoria Falls where the full width of the Zambezi River plummets off the fractured basalt plateau, tumbling into the base of the First Gorge one thousand feet below. The steel bridge spanning the Second Gorge was built in 1905 and was designed to be part of Cecil Rhodes' Cape to Cairo Railway.

Namibia

Crossing the border into the town of Katima, we are struck by how neat and orderly everything is in Namibia compared to where we've been for the last few months. Venturing westerly along the Caprivi Strip, we camp in the Mudumu National Park, beside the Kwando (or Cuando) River. The river rises in the central plains of Angola, flowing southeasterly to the Linyanti Swamp in Botswana. We camp in a remote part of the park, beside the river, and in the falling light, we watch a herd of elephant cross in front of us. From the matriarch down to the calf, their trunks poke from the water like periscopes. When they reach our side, they vanish silently among the trees.

During our few days in Windhoek, we learn the orderliness witnessed at the border is beginning to crack in the capital city. In a shop selling candles, the courteous lady owner warns us to be wary of the taxi touts. 'Zey're all crooks,' she declares. She came here from West Germany forty years ago, and so she knows a thing or two about this former German colonial town.

'Never flag zem down,' she cries, looking us up and down. 'Zey vill strip you of everysing... right down to your unterhosen.'

THE ORIGIN of the wild horses of the Namib may have something to do with Duwisib Castle, the former home of Hans Heinrich von Wolf. Von Wolf was a German officer serving in the *Schutztruppe* during the 1904 Herero uprising. Returning home to Germany following the cessation of hostilities, von Wolf married Miss Jayta Humphreys, the stepdaughter of the US consul. After marrying, they immediately returned to settle in German South-West Africa, buying twenty thousand hectares in the region south of Maltahöhe. He began breeding horses (as well as Hereford cattle, Merino sheep, and donkeys), and by 1911, he had three hundred and fifty horses roaming the property. At the outbreak of the First World War, von Wolf and his wife returned to Germany, though he was killed at the Front shortly after signing up. Jayta never returned to the castle, and shortly after the war, it became bankrupt, being bought by a Swedish owner (who was killed in World War Two), finally passing to the state in 1979. Might the property have been cursed?

Some four hundred kilometres south of Windhoek, the red sandstone, angular and turreted castle materialises from this semi-desert landscape, appearing remarkably out of place. The red stone was sourced locally, though all other materials and the workers came from Europe. We park by the cluster of camel thorn trees and make our way inside. With much of the furniture removed, it made for one of those curious discoveries that had been the flavour of our journey.

The more accepted explanation for the origin of the wild horses is that they are descendants of the Kubub stud farm that once existed in south-west Namibia, between Aus and Lüderitz, and abandoned during the First World War. At one time hidden from general view, because of their location within the restricted-access diamond mining area known as the Sperrgebiet, they only became more visible as a tourist attraction in the 1980s, when certain areas within the Sperrgebiet were included in the Namib-Naukluft Park.

The horses have clearly adapted to these conditions, helped by having access to troughs fed by various boreholes, deep shafts bored down to the water table. We watch them approach across the seemingly lifeless plain, from beyond the distorted, rust-coloured hills on the horizon. They throw their wild manes, kick and nip, pairs rearing in a challenging display of hooves. They might live a freer existence than their more domesticated cousins, but for all their display of bravado, they are just as prone to enjoying a stroke on the nose.

South Africa

Our arrival at the South African border, in effect, marks the end of our safari. From here, it is a blast along the coastal road to Cape Town. As if to confirm that we are entering a more prosperous country, not long after leaving the customs control behind us, a gleaming red Ferrari sports car races up the road towards us.

9

THE MAD MASSEUR OF MIDELT

2005

This bright sunlight is murder on the hangover, so I've retreated to the shade of a palm tree while I wait for Blair's taxi to whisk him from Malaga airport.

It's taken me four days to ride from France's Cote d'Azur to where I'm standing, Benalmadena Costa, southern Spain. The Honda Africa Twin has many attributes, but comfort is not one of them. Last night, on a section of road to Malaga, I was overtaken by a car with a sizeable dog squeezed into the trailer behind it. As he gazed at me from between the bars, his pink tongue lolled between open jaws, and each time the trailer hit a bump, his ears flapped. By then, I'd have swapped places with that dog for anything.

When Blair arrives, we retrieve his motorbike from a private lockup. I notice he's got some pretty natty luggage, which he fastens to the bike with a selection of webbing and clips. In no time, he's ready for the off. It's obvious which one of us is the Royal Marine. I'm feeling a little upstaged, because I've put my battered Nike bag inside a plastic bin liner and smothered it with frayed bungee straps. My luggage has all the appearance of being devoured by an anorexic octopus.

On the road, the weather is warm and sunny, and the flow of traffic unceasing. Meccano-like cranes outnumber the trees on this stretch of the coastline, and I ponder how the developers manage to sell all these properties, rising from the parched earth like broken grave stones.

Finally, Gibraltar looms sharply in the distance, the outline of Morocco's Rif Mountains beyond. My heart drums a little faster when I see them. What adventure awaits us beyond those distant peaks?

Within minutes of arriving at Algeciras port we have our tickets and are boarding the ferry. Crossing the Straits is quick, and, in the Spanish enclave of Ceuta, we make our way to the Parador and a comfortable night's sleep.

THE NEXT MORNING'S border crossing into Morocco is uneventful – the usual crowd, shuffling us from one queue to the next and all the while brimming with advice and an eye to the main chance. Everyone has a hand in your pocket. Best to go with the flow.

My first impressions are of how the country has tidied itself up since my last visit. Smart beachfront developments now feature on the road to Tetouan. Men are sweeping the streets, and a ring road encircles a town that once seemed to pride itself on the number of hustlers skulking among its alleyways.

Stopping by the roadside for a bite to eat, we quickly become a curiosity. It's Ramadan – the time of fasting. A man complains of being so thirsty his head hurts. I hide my apple by my side and offer him a cigarette.

'I cannot eat, drink, smoke or have sex until the sun sets,' he moans, slipping a couple of smokes into his shirt pocket for later. I feel a suitable proverb coming on: 'He with the biggest pockets will be most bountiful by nightfall.' I keep it to myself.

On the southern outskirts of Meknes, where we take a couple of rooms at Hotel Zaki, the guard has us drive the bikes up the front steps, assuring us they'll be safe next to the potted plants.

'I hope we're going to do some camping,' Blair mutters.

I pretend not to hear him.

TODAY THE SKY is a clear blue. At El Ksiba, we take fuel and follow the road to Imilchil, climbing above the plains. As the sun drops, we pull off the road into woodland and make camp. We had hoped to arrive undetected, when a shepherd boy passes with his flock. With a small fire going, Blair strikes up his stove, and we feast on military ration packs – pork casserole, followed by chocolate sponge.

It's very quiet in these foothills, save for a light wind rustling the branches. Our position among the trees appears secure. However, I create a defensive position by forming a low boma of branches around our bivouac. In the falling light, I keep the night scopes close to hand, slipping the Guardian Angel pepper spray into my belt. Blair holsters the eight-round magazine of mini rocket flares. We're larking over whether it was wise to have allowed the shepherd boy his freedom when there's a rustling beyond the firelight and the sound of voices.

We've been clocked!

Before I can reach for the night scopes, we're confronted by four men and two youths. The shepherd boy is among them looking, dare I say… rather sheepish.

Blair and I exchange glances when the man with a craggy face slips his hand beneath a white cloth, shrouding something he's holding in front of his chest. His lips twist into a grin. Firelight dances on their hewn features. I make a rapid appraisal of our firepower. My pepper spray is capable of firing two charges – good enough to whack the man with the cloth. I rely on Blair to slot the others. I crouch forward, hand hovering by the Guardian Angel.

Then, it happens in a flash.

With a deft flick of his wrist, Craggy Features sends the white cloth whirling into the night sky, revealing nothing more threatening than a tray containing a silver tea pot and glasses.

'Bloody hell!'

If Jeeves ever morphed into a pixie, then this was him, grinning from ear to ear in a wood in Morocco.

Next to the teapot lies a circular loaf of bread. Aha! I want to tell Blair it's a charm offensive before closing for the kill, but I don't wish my frivolous humour to insult our visitors. Somewhat overwhelmed, we politely refuse the tea and bread, until we finally put away our silly Western manners and tuck in.

As we tear off chunks of bread and slurp the tea, our little group settles round the fire. The two youths are sent to fetch more wood. I cringe as they destroy my carefully constructed boma, throwing it, branch by painstakingly collected branch, on the fire. We converse in short Arabic phrases from a guidebook, slipping in the odd French word along the way. The mint tea is excellent. So is the bread. We pass a very pleasant hour, and when they depart for the evening, they leave us with the rest of the bread and a memorable experience.

By three in the morning, I discover my sleeping bag is way too thin for these mountain conditions. And my head is cold. I must remember a woolly hat for next time. The sky is awash with stars.

Sunrise is at six. I warm my hands against the fire. Dogs bark in the distance. Breakfast is sausage and beans... and the pixie's bread. As we pack, the shepherd boy herds his flock into camp, leaving me wondering if he wants to sell us one. Sorry, mate. No room for a sheep.

The road to Imilchil is now all tarmac. We pass the two lakes on the plateau, Iseli and Tislit – my third such visit. Not much ever changes here. The waters are still, reflecting the surrounding landscape and the blue sky. A good omen for our journey.

At the turning to Rich, the route becomes broken rock and dirt. It's heavy going and slow, and we pass through the occasional village, witnessing the simple lifestyles they lead up here. By Ait Hani we're back on tarmac for the fast, twisty stretch to the Todra Gorge.

In Tinerhir, we stay at Kasbah Lamrani, parking our bikes within the security of its walls. I head straight for the pool, while Blair completes his 'administration', military code for washing his socks and undies. The pool is unspeakably cold. I manage two widths of it before warming myself over a chilled beer.

The concierge tells us our planned route through the mountains is not possible by motorcycle. He gives us his brother's address in Taghbalt, advising us to call on him if we have any problems.

. . .

We take fuel and water and head south across the plains from Tinerhir. In the distance rise the Jebel Sarhro mountains. The sky clouds over, and it gets cooler as we head higher. The track is made of dirt and rocks, and we're careful to preserve the tyres as best we can. We eventually crest Tizzi-n-Tazzazert pass at an altitude of two thousand two hundred metres. Since I was last here, a café has been built at the viewing point.

'If someone goes to the effort of building a café all the way up here, we should at least have a drink,' Blair reasons.

The lady of the house serves us tea and an excellent omelette. Her name is Ishmael. A little boy talks incessantly in the background and chases a bicycle tyre. A shy girl dressed in bright, traditional costume, her face veiled, is perched on a rock. It transpires she's waiting by the track for a husband to come by. I wonder how long she's been here, speculating whether she could be the girl I bought the Jebel Sarhro rock from some five years before.

'Why don't you take her?' suggests Brahim, the husband of Ishmael.

'We already have wives,' I counter, content such a statement will conclude the matter.

He laughs at me. 'She could be your woman in Morocco.'

Blair snatches up his plate. 'Can I have another omelette?'

Judging by the crease on Ishmael's forehead, I suspect she's never served two omelettes in a row to the same person. Thankfully, the subject of marriage is immediately forgotten.

'You can stay for the night,' Ishmael offers when it starts

to rain. She sets down the fresh plate of food in front of Blair. 'You can stay in one of the huts.'

We take up the offer and then go for a walk, visiting a nomad and his family on the next hill. He has two wives and umpteen children, and he looks happy enough. Good for him. They make us tea and bread while we shelter from the wind behind a low stone wall.

Our hut, constructed from rock and mud, is very cosy and has rugs and sleeping mats on the floor. Blair goes off to find a quiet corner to meditate while I read a book with the aid of my head torch. After a while, Brahim pokes his head in. For a moment, he just stares at me.

'Why are you lying on the floor with a light on your head?' he asks, flicking the light switch adjacent to the door. The bulb flickers and then emits a subdued glow.

'I'm trying to save your batteries,' I tell him. He looks perplexed.

Outside, I hear Blair's footsteps returning. 'Why were you sleeping in the shower?' Ishmael challenges him.

There's a pause. 'I was meditating,' I hear Blair explain, though I can tell he's on a hiding to nothing. I guess they think we're rather odd.

Ishmael cooks a pretty good tagine for us, and then we hit the sack. It's very quiet up here.

WE RISE EARLY to catch the sunrise, though a light cloud hangs in the east. The harsh, arid landscape of conical hills is cast in a patchwork of light and shadow. For breakfast, we have another omelette and then trundle down the mountain to Nekob. The track is rocky and slow going all the way, which sets me thinking: there were no chickens at Brahim's place and I marvel at how he gets the eggs up this road in one piece. Could that be why his wife only makes omelettes?

After Nekob, we take the tarmac to Tazzarine, before heading south-east to Tarhbalt. From here, we pick up the track that joins with the Merzouga–Zagora piste. As we search for the start of the track, a bunch of guys are frantic to act as our guides. We head off across a stony plain with two blokes on bicycles hot on our heels. It must be 30C plus, and it's beyond all reason why they follow us in this heat. We stop after a couple of kilometres and consult our maps. Within moments, the two cyclists buzz around us again, glistening in sweat. It's incredible what lengths these guys will go to close a sale. Except we just don't need them to guide us over this desert plain. We give them a few coins and head off.

The only vehicles we encounter along the way are three French 4x4s. They advance towards us from the shimmering distance, all knobbly tyres and whirling dust, cotton scarves flying from open windows. We pull off the track so as not to become a part of the scenery. They judder to a halt and leap from their vehicles, a veritable whirlwind of movement. 'Yes, we're on the right track for Zagora,' they confirm, and after a few more exchanges, their tyres are once more ripping rock, and they're off, heading in the direction of the two mad cyclists.

We drop off the escarpment and point east. The track is firm sand, the occasional soft patch sending us slithering every which way. Finally, it turns to rock. All too soon, and the sun is touching the horizon, dusk soon upon us. Finding our way in the dark is not so easy, and even though the lights of Zagora shine in the distance, we take the wrong track for a while. I'm beginning to wonder if we might have to spend the night out here, when a cluster of palm trees and a settlement of small, square huts materialises. Tourists mounted on camels lope from the gloom. I can't for the life of me imagine where they're going at this time of night. The dust hangs like an impenetrable fog.

We press on until a kasbah-style hotel, the Palais Asmaa, emerges majestically from the murk. There are already several motorcycles parked outside, and it proves not a bad place to rest up for the night.

On the road to M'Hamid, we stop in Tagounite to purchase our customary lunch of cheese and bread. We have in mind to do a photo shoot down at the dunes – a *Lawrence of Arabia* meets *Easy Rider* kind of affair.

M'Hamid is the end of the road, beyond which lies hundreds of kilometres of sand. We cruise the southern outskirts of this ramshackle town in search of suitable dunes for our photos. There are plenty of them in the distance, yet neither of us can muster the urge to bash through the deep sand to reach them. We're looking for something a little more accessible. We backtrack until we find a mound of sand close to the road. For the best effect, I lie face down on the roadside, snapping a picture of Blair, water bottle in hand, clawing his way over this inhospitable landscape – looking exceptionally healthy.

Making an early morning ride to Foum Zguid, we stock up on food, water and fuel before riding out of town on the piste to Akka-Irhen. We're using notes from Chris Scott's guidebook *Sahara Overland*, though attempting the route in the reverse direction to Chris's very precise GPS references, which doesn't help the navigation. I lead with the aid of preprogrammed waypoints in the GPS, though I don't enter every single one. I just can't believe we need them all.

The plain is a mishmash of tracks, eventually directing us into a dry river of deep silt. Despite being off course, we make the first waypoint (within fifty metres) and pass through a village. We don't know it yet, but I've just taken the wrong track out.

We plough merrily on, the wheel tracks ahead of us less clear now, even though the pointer on the GPS suggests all is well. We come out on a rocky plain, passing a couple of nomads' tents. The track fades, and we're back in deep silt, where plenty of throttle sees us through it.

We follow camel tracks until ending up in a boulder field, feet paddling either side to keep the bikes upright. Blair's bike becomes wedged on a rock, and we must heave it off. This can't be right. We stop to consult the map. By studying the contours, we conclude that our position puts us the wrong side of a ridge of hills to our right – we have not taken enough care to read the contours of the land and match them to the map.

Together, we walk for twenty minutes over the boulder field to see if we can determine a way through. In the forty-minute round trip, I consume another litre of water. Quenching my thirst is akin to dousing a fire. We have lunch in the sliver of shade provided by a lone tree, convincing ourselves we could most likely get through. Nevertheless, in these conditions, our rate of water consumption is too high, and the supplies already well depleted. I'm also concerned about breaking bones on these rocks. I don't fancy the chances of a medevac from here. Our telephones don't work, and I never did get the hang of smoke signals. I'm not even sure who might see them.

Reluctantly, we return the way we've come, getting

disorientated in the process and losing our original track. The main road runs due west, and we use this as our reference point, reaching it without further complications.

A fine lesson in the perils of desert navigation has just been rammed firmly home.

A sandstorm passes through as we head back to our previous night's camp by the dry river. It's raining, the dust turning to mud, and we stand beneath a palm while the worst of it blows through.

I curse my petrol cooker: a covering of greasy soot on my hands goes all over my trousers, the cooking utensils, the pan, the food, the bike. Oh, the joys of camping.

'You'll feel better after a good meal.' says Blair.

The rain stops as we eat and within no time the ground is dry again. I fall into my scrape and sleep for ten blissful hours.

FROM GOULMIMA, we make the short ride to Midelt, breaking for breakfast at a café in Er Richidia. The weather has turned distinctly chilly, not helped by the strong wind. The road climbs to an altitude of two thousand metres before dropping away, and it's a relief to catch sight of the Hotel Kasbah Asmaa on the approach to Midelt. Inside, there is a roaring fire in the hearth. We throw our gear into our rooms and head into town for the usual diet of bread and cheese.

'You want a hotel?' the man outside the shop asks us. 'I find you a good hotel in Midelt.'

'Thanks,' I say. 'We're sorted at the Kasbah.'

'Come with me to the hammam,' he presses. 'Very good massage at the hammam.'

Blair is rolling his shoulders, lips pursed. 'You know, my back is quite stiff.'

The man's rubbing his hands. 'Very good massage at the—'

'Thanks,' I butt in. 'He'll live. No hammam today.'

I go and buy the bread and cheese, and when I get back outside, Blair has arranged an appointment for us both at three o'clock.

'Meet me at the café,' the man is saying, and with that, he vanishes.

We return to the hotel to eat our lunch. The cheese is especially cloying, and I attempt the difficult feat of eating and speaking simultaneously. 'You've seen... what they did to Ewan McGregor... in that hammam in Kazakhstan... and I've got a bad back.' I sense my gums gradually seizing with the effort. 'I don't want any masseur... messing with my back.'

Blair slaps another slab of cheese on some bread. 'If he comes on a bit rough, just tell him to bugger off!'

'I bloody will,' I say, swatting crumbs from my shirt and sauntering off to my room. 'Besides, I've a lot of administration to do.'

There's no plug in this sink, and I have a mountain of washing. I studiously wash each sock, turning them inside out before continuing, determined they'll be the cleanest socks in all of Morocco. There's no chance I'll be ready by three o'clock.

At the stroke of three, we're back at the bar in Midelt. It seems nobody has heard of Nadir. I smirk. Thank God for that. 'You mean Nordine!' shouts a man at the end of the bar. Damn!

In no time, Nordine arrives, and we head off across waste

ground and into the suburbs of Midelt, following one dusty alley after another.

'This is it,' Nordine declares, and we venture into a shabby, grey building.

In the changing room, we undress to our underpants, grab a bucket and enter the first chamber. It's warm. A man raises a sponge from a bucket, squeezing the water over his chest. We enter a second chamber. It's warmer still. A couple of guys look to have been discarded against the wall. They give the impression of being close to death. A wall of steam marks the entrance to the third chamber. I step inside, tentatively drawing a breath of burning heat. I head for the source of water spewing from the wall, hopping from one scalded foot to the other. Nordine snatches my bucket, telling me to go sit in the far corner, where the tiles are marginally cooler. I lie out, gradually sensing the tension drip from my shoulders. Nordine brings me the bucket, and I use the cup to ladle the steaming water over my head. Yes, this'll do just fine. All is well.

Though not for long.

A weasel of a man converges on me from the mist. He has an evil grin and a ribcage that could double as a toast rack. A bony finger beckons. 'What is your name?' he crows, in perfect English. I tell him. 'Come with me.'

Nordine is grinning expectantly. Blair grunts as an athletic-looking chap twists his legs into unspeakable angles.

This weasel is not getting on my back. No way. I'll chuck him across the hammam if he tries any fancy moves.

No sooner am I laid face down than he drops his full weight on me, his knees gouging savagely. Several joints pop in my spine. The air is punched from my lungs, and I'm rendered speechless. The bloody fool must think I'm made of modelling clay.

'Relax!' he cries, shaking an arm like a terrier kills a rat. The snap of cracking joints echoes off the vaulted ceiling. I groan. He takes my knackered right knee, twisting it into a position it hasn't known for years.

'You can't do that,' I blubber.

'Relax!'

Thoroughly steamed and pummelled, I emerge into the sunlight feeling pretty good. Blair's looking smug. 'I told you it would do you some good.'

'Smart-arse.'

We take mint tea with Nordine at a roadside café, and then we go to the family house of his girlfriend, who has laid on more tea and pastries, Moroccan specialities that I am in danger of rather rudely wolfing down. Later, he asks us for dinner with his brother and mother, who cooks us all an excellent couscous.

After we say goodnight to Nordine and take our taxi back to the hotel, I feel a little ashamed of how offhandedly I tried to dismiss him earlier in the day. He wanted nothing more than our company and for us to know he was there for the future – just in case we could do some business. In the clamour of the hard sell, which is so often the way in this country, it is possible to miss gems like Nordine.

We check the bikes and discover a nail embedded in Blair's rear tyre. The Ultra-Seal product we've filled the tyres with does a fine job of immediately sealing the hole when I pull the nail out.

. . .

It freezes overnight with fresh snow lying on the higher ground. The bikes are covered in frost. I put on as many layers as possible under the riding suit.

We have a long run ahead of us, so I partially inflate the sleeping mat and strap it to the seat. It dramatically improves the comfort, provided I don't overinflate it, which has the effect of raising me higher above the screen and the increased impact from the wind.

We stop in Guercif for a lunch of lamb and chips, which makes a nice change from cheese and bread. The ferry is not until 22:00 hours, so by late afternoon, we head out across the Plaine de Gareb to rest up in the low hills. Firing up the stove, we cook the last of our military rations – chicken and dumplings followed by treacle sponge. Excellent.

Chaos reigns at the ferry terminal. I persuade Blair that it's my turn to guard the bikes and watch him march determinedly into the terminal.

'Obtaining the boarding pass was a war of attrition,' he says, looking a tad harassed when he returns.

The ferry to Almeria in Spain is pretty rusty. A film of sand coats the alleyways. Our shared cabin is so small we have to throw our luggage into the cabin from the door and then take it in turns to climb over it to reach the bunks. The clamour of noise outside the cabin door is constant. I focus my mind on the camp in the shade of the palms, beside the dry river on the edge of the desert, remote and tranquil. Very soon, I'm fast asleep.

10

JOHN'S LAST SAFARI

2002. Damaraland, Namibia

It was late afternoon, and the heat was crippling. I nosed the Toyota into the shade of a tree next to the parched riverbed. The campsite staff had already chopped a selection of wood, placing it next to our barbeque: a low, three-sided construction of stones with a blackened grill on top.

'The shower is over there.' Robert, the man who ran the camp, pointed to a thatched roof poking above some bushes. 'I'll make the fire at six. Then you'll have hot water.'

About fifty metres from us stood a blue Land Rover, an awning pegged by its side cast shade over three chairs and a table. There was a tent on its roof.

For several minutes we plodded around, stretching stiff limbs after the long, hot drive from Swakopmund.

Before long, a man and two women came by. The man held back while the two women continued to the blue Land Rover, slumping into the chairs in the shade of the awning.

'Hi,' the man said, ambling towards us. He was from

Manchester, England, and asked us where we'd come from that day. For a moment, we exchanged useful bush intelligence.

'You've been up to see the engravings?' I enquired.

'Nah. We've been up on the rocks, over there. It's a beautiful place.' He'd inclined his head towards the Land Rover, and his next words were spoken in barely more than a whisper. 'Diana lost her husband this year. We've spread his ashes up there. It's what John always wanted.'

I'd gazed up at the rocks after the man had gone, tempted to climb up there. Maybe tomorrow morning, I reasoned. When it's cooler.

I went to join Christine and our friend Sabine, who were resting in the shade of the tree. I laid down, shutting my eyes, wondering what I might find up there on the rocks. This is the story that came to mind.

~

THE HEAT IS STIFLING up here on the rocks, even though the sun, its force spent, edges over the horizon. I hold the camera tightly in my left hand, using the other to steady myself as I climb the last metre or two to the plateau.

I'm a little late. Undoubtedly, the best light has already gone. In the distance, the mountains are a dark silhouette against the orange sky. I can see that now I've reached the top. Where the shadows end, the sun catches the long grasses. The tips sway, luminous, like woven gold. In the foreground, sandstone boulders glow as if the embers of an immense fire.

I stroll to the edge of the rock, smelling the sweet pipe smoke lingering in the dry air. And then I see him, sitting alone just below the lip, absolutely still. I catch the back of his head first, the cropped hair greying at the temples, and, as I draw closer, the khaki shirt stretched over broad shoulders. I tread soundlessly, not wishing to disturb his moment with the closing day or to alarm him.

As I approach, his head and shoulders turn slowly to face me. He nods. The evening light softens the ageing, drawn features. In that instant, I sense he's known all along I'm here.

'You've missed the best,' he announces.

'It's too hot. I couldn't set out earlier.'

'Must have been nigh on fifty today.'

I drop to my haunches, sitting on the lip of the warm rock. I lift the camera, observing through the lens how the sun illuminates the streaks of high cloud in a particular way, their edges reflecting a thin strip of vibrant colour, as if they are slashes in an artist's canvas. The camera clicks as I snatch the image.

The man speaks softly when he says, 'You won't capture such vitality. I never did, and I used to come here whenever I could. Just to be here was always so very invigorating. It cleanses the soul. You know, I used to imagine I could sense the spirit of the San people.' His right arm rises to describe an arc. 'They're out there. This is their country. They were here before anyone.'

The San, a diverse group of hunter-gatherers, have lived in Southern Africa for more than twenty thousand years. After a long silence, I, too, imagine I sense their spirit: a feeling of inner peace, of great calm. I can't be very sure what external force, if any, influences that.

'From what I've seen in life...' the man breaks off for a second. 'I believe there is much we could learn from these people. And yet, what is quite astonishing is how inferior we consider them. It is a sad reflection if we can only find peace in a wilderness, don't you think?'

The man strikes a match, puts the pipe to his mouth and puts the match to the bowl. His lips click as he sucks on the stem, blowing out a blue cloud of smoke. He places the extinguished match in the breast pocket of his shirt.

'You know, it's said that in San lore, at the beginning of time, the human and the animal world all lived together in harmony beneath the surface of the earth. It's said they lived in the light, despite the fact there was no sun. Then Kaang, Lord of All Life, began to plan the world above and to put on the surface of that world all the trees and the rivers, the mountains and the plains. When he'd finished, he wanted to share such a creation, and so he dug a deep hole at the base of a big tree, and he brought up the first man, and then the first woman, until all the people were gathered. Then he brought up all the animals, and when they were all together, he instructed them to live in peace, warning the people never to build any fires, for if they did, a great evil would befall them. They gave their word, and Kaang left for a place from where he could watch over them.' The man gently taps the bowl of the pipe with his finger. 'Then, as evening approached and the sun began to sink below the mountains, the people and the animals watched in wonder at this strange happening. Before long, fear crept into the hearts of the people, for they could no longer see in the dark as the animals could, and they had no fur on their backs to keep them warm. They set aside Kaang's warning and made a fire. Soon they were warm and could see each other again.

'The fire, however, frightened the animals, and they fled into the caves and the mountains, and ever since they broke Kaang's command, fear has replaced friendship between people and animals.'

After a moment, the man glances towards me, his silvery brows arched. He clamps the pipe between his teeth.

'I suppose we'll always acquire power at our peril,' I say. 'I imagine it'll never change.'

'Let's hope we never lose places like this, then. Let's hope we don't frighten away the spirits, at least.'

'Yes. That would be too sad.'

The shadows are growing long now, stealthily cloaking the plain. After a while I get to my feet and collect up my camera. 'I'm heading back to camp,' I tell him. 'Are you staying?'

'Oh yes.' The man rasps a finger over his cheek. 'I'll be here a good while.'

'Thank you for the story.'

The man doesn't look round. He raises his hand in a gesture of farewell and holds it there a moment. I turn and walk away.

It's early when we leave camp the next day, and already the heat is crushing.

At the entrance to the camp, on the bank of a dry river, is the wooden hut where the staff shelter from the sun. They are under an awning of corrugated tin, and above it is the name: The Wilderness Camp. I stop the Toyota and stroll to the hut.

The camp manager's name is Robert, and next to him is a young girl, her hair braided with coloured beads. She casts me shy glances.

Robert breaks into an easy smile. 'How was your stay?' he asks.

I point to the sign above the awning. 'You gave it the right name, that's for sure.'

'Oh yeah.' He beams. 'Maybe you heard the jackal last night. He was calling.'

'I heard him.' I peel off the notes we owe Robert for our night's stay and hand them over.

He folds them, places the bundle in a battered metal box and closes the lid. 'Please, I would like you to sign the guest-book before you leave.'

I slide it over the table towards me, taking the chewed biro from Robert's outstretched hand. I read the last entry in the book – *John's last safari. There is no place he loved more than here. Rest in Peace.*

I hold the pen above where I intend to write. 'Who was John?' I enquire.

Robert points across the river, in the direction of the track leading from camp. 'He died this year. His friends, they just left in that blue Land Rover.'

'They were next to us in camp,' I tell him, recalling the two women and their male companion.

Robert nods, and some of the sparkle evaporates. 'John was coming here for years. Yesterday, they put his ashes high on the rock beyond the trees. He was always up there. He was a nice man. Sometimes, when I go up there to watch the sunset, I think I can still smell the smoke from his pipe.'

I shiver despite the heat. I know it is the most ridiculous question: 'Have you ever seen him up there?'

Robert is laughing now. 'Oh man, no way. I only smell his pipe. He used to ask me to sit with him and tell him the stories of the San. He liked to hear about Kaang making the moon from an old shoe, and how a man can become the spirit of an animal. He liked to talk about those myths.' Robert rubs his shiny cheek thoughtfully. 'Perhaps he was the jackal we heard last night.'

11

WHY DO GOATS CLIMB TREES?

2006

The air is cool, the sun having not yet risen above the minaret. Women bustle their children to school along the cobbled street, weaving between the rabble of eagle-eyed men. A spare-looking donkey parts the crowd, tugging a creaking cart overflowing with rubble. A butcher has thrown open his shutters to display dark, marbled intestines sprawled on a wooden counter. Beyond the archway, unshaven taxi drivers languish next to their battered vehicles. The nauseating exhaust fumes from over-revved scooters hang in the air.

I've learnt to avert my gaze, to engage anything but these men intent on grasping our attention. I'm not seeking to offend. Or be impolite. I'm merely being practical. If we are to be drawn by every soul who wishes to gain our attention, it will be impossible to progress any further than this next telegraph post, on which the storks have precariously perched their nest. It is as if we emit the scent of wounded animals. We might as well bear placards announcing, 'Newly arrived'.

Christine has been snared by a fellow selling a book about the palaces of Marrakech. She's very polite. Perhaps, a little too polite. It takes five minutes to untangle the web he's weaving. Another chap, dressed in a blue shirt and jeans, is exceptionally persistent about visiting a Berber craft centre. A battle of attrition commences. We are finally won over, following him through a doorway and along a short corridor.

We find ourselves inside a pharmacist, the shelves crammed with glass jars containing a psychedelic mix of powders and liquids. It's not quite the Berber crafts we'd had in mind. The female attendant begins by explaining the more obscure products in stock. She reaches for a jar packed with what appear to be sticks of liquorice. She shoves one under my nose. It seems most of their products are best appreciated with a sharp intake of air.

'This is very good for making whoopee,' the lady announces. 'Boil it for ten minutes in water, drink the liquid immediately and then straight to bed with woman.'

She cackles as she presses the stalk firmly into my palm. It's not clear why she thinks I'm in need of 'whoopee'. Perhaps I appear a little tense after our encounters in the street.

I turn away when she swings an opened bottle of rose water toward Christine. And it's then I catch sight of the framed photograph hanging on the wall, instantly igniting the memory of a crowd of rowdy friends gathered round the lunch table, jugs of sangria, half-eaten bowls of salad, discarded plates and an army of glasses. In this moment, it's as if I float above the scene, observing the fun.

'I'm telling you, it's a fact that goats climb trees,' someone said.

'Have you ever seen a goat in a tree?' another replied.

'Do you have a photograph?'

'Why would a goat even climb a tree?'

And so, the drunken reverie continued for much of the afternoon. Why, indeed, might a goat climb a tree? None of the other diners in the restaurant could answer such a question. This is why, two months later, three of us found ourselves trundling up a dusty track in the Anti-Atlas, bent on a quest to uncover this mystery.

It was the most appallingly planned foray I've ever undertaken. Other than a rough idea of the region we should head for, I possessed no clue of where we might begin our search, which meant the four days I'd allocated demanded every minute of daylight be spent pursuing our goal. With so little information to hand, we would gather intelligence en route. Simple as that. Christine would be our linguist. Paul, our chief mechanic.

'We'll be staying in hotels, I presume?' Paul had chirped hopefully down the phone before leaving for the airport.

'Absolutely,' I replied, having just forced a brand new, three-person tent into the Suzuki jeep.

Three days later, as the sun started falling over the Moroccan landscape, we found ourselves in a secluded valley in the province of Ouazzane.

'Not many hotels round here,' mumbled Paul, looking about him. 'Not much of anything, in fact.'

He was spot on there.

We pulled off the road beside a voluminous hedge and slipped the newly acquired tent from its protective cover. That was when I discovered the package contained not a single peg or pole, though by then, we were far too tired to get creative, so we laid like sardines on the hard earth, pulling the tent up to our chins. The material crackled each time one of us turned, and by morning, our heads were sodden with dew. By sun-up, we were back on the trail.

All of that day, our quarry eluded us. From time to time, Christine hopped from the car with the burning question, 'Where can we find the goats in the trees?'

Always it was answered with the same nonchalant flick of the hand, 'Go south,' they told us. 'Follow the rising sun.'

And so, we did, until arriving in the foothills of the mountains. By then, Paul had resigned himself to the fact that his nights would not be spent reclining on a soft hotel mattress, and so that evening, he set about stringing the tent from between the back door of the jeep and a nearby tree. In the dead of night, he shot bolt upright.

'There's a great big animal trying to get in this tent,' he whispered.

'Go outside and shoo it away,' I murmured.

'Not likely.'

In the morning, the tiny scrape marks of a rodent were the only evidence of Paul's 'great big animal'.

We headed ever higher into the mountains, following the rising sun. In a lush valley, we saw a herd of goats some way in the distance. The shepherd was sitting on a rock watching over them. Not a single one of them was in a tree.

'Go and ask the shepherd if we can stick one of his goats in a tree,' Paul suggested to Christine. 'At least then we can take a photo of it and clear off home.'

Before we could implement such a plan, the shepherd herded his flock over the distant hill. Our cunning plan foiled, we drove on, heading higher and higher, while more and more of the grey dust from the track coated every conceivable surface in the car.

'I hate to point out the blindingly obvious,' Christine said, 'but the higher we go, the fewer trees there are.'

We stopped for a moment to savour this nugget of truth.

'Eventually, we shall go down the other side,' I reasoned.

'Only the desert lies on the other side.'

We sat in the car, pondering our next move. A warm breeze brushed through the open windows. There was silence save for the crackle of burning tobacco in Christine's cigarette.

PLOP!

'What's that smell?' Paul asked.

'Petrol,' I said.

PLOP!

'Where's it coming from?'

I looked up to see a dark stain on the jeep's fibreglass roof, a drip slowly forming in the centre of it. I gawped at Christine's burning cigarette.

PLOP!

'The fuel tank on the roof's leaking,' I howled. 'Quick! Throw out the cigarette.'

We bailed from the car in a shroud of dust and flailing limbs, hitting the ground before the cigarette did. On closer inspection, the roof rack had worn a small hole through the base of the spare fuel tank. We could no longer cross the mountains, even if we wanted to.

'We need to go around them,' I proposed.

That night's campsite was among thick shrubbery beside a busy roundabout outside Marrakech. After the traffic noise disrupted our sleep, I sensed the beginnings of a mutiny among the crew. I couldn't afford to lose both my linguist and my chief mechanic. Our quest needed modifying.

'Perhaps we should head back north,' I suggested. 'There must be some tree goats in the north.'

'Agreed,' they chorused. 'Let's go north.'

On the plains above Ksar-el-Kebir, an old man in a military trench coat brought us to a halt with an authoritative hand. 'Where are you going?' he demanded.

'We're looking for goats in trees.'

He shook his head. 'You must go south. You must follow the rising sun.'

'Yes. We know.' We thanked him for his advice, offered him a cigarette and continued north.

'It's a myth, this goat thing,' I said.

'You could be right.'

Over the next hill, our spirits rose when we caught sight of a flock of goats. There were brown ones, black ones, white ones, mixed-coloured ones. Some small, some a bit larger. It was, I believed, a veritable representation of all things Capra hircus. None of them, however, displayed the slightest inkling of climbing any of the many trees.

'Okay,' I pronounced, bringing the jeep to a juddering stop. 'There's nothing left to do but employ a little reverse logic.'

'Let's keep that simple, shall we,' Paul said, shooting me a distrustful glance.

I climbed from the car, sweeping a hand over our surroundings. 'You see these trees all around us?'

'Yes. We see them.'

'And all these goats?'

'Yes.'

'There is not a single goat in any one of these trees, right?'

'Agreed. Not one of them.'

'Ergo, goats don't climb trees.' I puffed out my chest, strutting back to the jeep.

'Brilliant!'

'Can we go home now?' Paul asked.

'Therefore,' I continued, 'we must take a photograph as evidence of all these goats not climbing any of these trees. And yes, then we may return home with our unprecedented findings.'

I strode to the passenger window. 'Camera, please.'

Paul was frowning.

'What's the matter?'

'There's no film in it.'

'Impossible.'

'I'm telling you, there's no roll of film in the camera.'

'Damn!'

Perhaps I hadn't checked it before we left.

I SHAKE my head free from the memory of twenty years ago, my focus returning immediately to the pharmacist's shop and the photograph on the wall of a tree overburdened with foraging goats.

Christine is looking at me quizzically. 'What are you giggling at?' she presses. 'You're sitting there in your own little world.'

I point to the photo. 'Do you remember our quest to find the goats in trees?'

She takes a couple of steps closer to the photograph. 'How could I forget?'

'They are eating the fruit of the argan tree,' the pharmacist explains. 'Goats love this fruit. The problem is they get to it before the farmers have time to pick it. Then the farmers must gather the stones regurgitated or defecated by the goats.'

'What does the farmer want with the stones of the argan fruit?'

She reaches for a bottle containing a yellow liquid. 'The stones are crushed down and used for making cooking oil. Just like this one. It's quite expensive to buy in Europe. They also make a body cream from it. Would you like some?'

I shake my head, thinking I might skip on the cooking oil, too, if it's been through the digestive system of a goat.

'I'll settle for the whoopee stick,' I tell her.

THANK you for reading *Why Do Goats Climb Trees?*. I really hope you enjoyed the stories. Please consider leaving a review at Amazon or Goodreads. Leaving a review helps to place my book in front of other readers, which is of great benefit.

For news, articles and information on my other books, please join me at www.latitude14.com

All the best,

James

Printed in Great Britain
by Amazon

43285557R00108